SURVIVORS

BATTLEFIELD RELICS OF WWII

SURVIVORS
BATTLEFIELD RELICS OF WWII

SIMON & JONATHAN FORTY

CHARTWELL
BOOKS

This edition published in 2018 by Chartwell Books
an imprint of The Quarto Group
142 West 36th Street, 4th Floor
New York, NY 10018 USA
T (212) 779-4972 **F** (212) 779-6058
www.QuartoKnows.com

ISBN: 978-0-7858-3578-3

Printed and bound in China

10 9 8 7 6 5 4 3 2 1

Design: Greene Media Ltd/EF Design

Page 1: *Tiger I, Vimoutiers, France, 2017.* Unless specified, all modern photos were taken by the authors

Pages 2/3: *At the Mont Ormel memorial an M4A1(76) looks out over the killing ground of the Falaise Gap. It was here that Polish units fought to stop the German attempts to break out. (See p. 68.)*

This Page: *Churchill Crocodile outside the D-Day Museum, Portsmouth, UK. The bull's head marking denotes 79th Armoured Division. The flame-thrower replaced the hull MG and could fire 80 one-second bursts, the fuel coming from a trailer. Particularly effective against bunkers and fixed fortifications, 800 of this fearsome weapon had been produced by the end of the war.* Geni/WikiCommons/GFDL (CC-BY-SA)

Acknowledgments
Thanks to all those who provided material for this book. All photos are credited with their caption: apologies to anyone omitted. Thanks to Mark for line drawings; Piers for Russian translation; Richard Wood and Peter Anderson for help with photos. Anyone who is interested in this subject should look no further than the.shaddock. free.fr/Surviving_Panzers.html, preservedtanks.com, *and* www. tracesofwar.com. *Both sites are full of information and indispensible.*

Photo on page 153 courtesy NAC—National Digital Archives, Poland.

Contents

Glossary and Abbreviations

1er/2e DB French 1st/2nd Armored Divisions (Division Blindée).

1er DFL 1st Division Française Libre (Free French Division).

AA Antiaircraft.

AAMG Antiaircraft machine gun.

Abteilung German unit roughly equivalent to a battalion.

AFV Armored fighting vehicle.

AP Armor-piercing.

APC Armored personnel carrier.

APCBC Armor-piercing, capped, ballistic capped. Armor-piercing projectile that has a piercing cap over the nose to help prevent break-up when hitting angled, face-hardened armor. Aerodynamic ballistic caps were placed over the piercing caps.

APDS Armor-piercing discarding sabot. The projectile is smaller than the diameter of the gun's barrel and the space between the projectile and barrel wall is filled with a "sabot" (a French word for a shoe). This increases muzzle velocity.

APFSDS Armor-piercing fin-stabilized discarding sabot. These APDS projectiles were given aerodynamic stability through fold-out fins rather than being spun by the gun rifling.

Ausf *Ausführung* = model in German.

Armoured In unit designations, British spelling of armored indicates a British, Commonwealth, or Polish formation.

ARV Armored recovery vehicle = *Bergepanzer* in German.

AVLB Armored vehicle-launched bridge.

blindée Armored in French.

BT *Bystrokhodnyy Tank* = fast tank in Russian.

caliber (cal) The diameter of the bore of a gun barrel. Also used as a unit of length of a gun barrel. For example a 10in/20cal gun would have a barrel 200 inches long (10 x 20). This is specified in millimeters, centimeters, or inches depending on the historical period and national preference.

char Tank in French.

FA Field artillery.

GMC Gun motor carriage.

HB eg M2HB—heavy barrel, usually air-cooled and did not require a water jacket around the barrel for cooling.

HE High explosive.

HMC Howitzer motor carriage.

HVSS Horizontal volute spring suspension: this type

Below: *Imparting high velocity to projectiles.* Artwork by Mark Franklin.

Conventional gun firing lightweight full-diameter projectiles

Conventional gun firing APDS

Long gun firing conventional projectiles

Tapered-bore gun firing skirted projectiles

Conventional gun firing rocket-assisted projectiles

Methods of Penetrating Armor

APHE

Shell penetrates armor by force of impact

Shell explodes inside tank beyond armor

APBC

Bottom plate and ballistic cap are destroyed; hardened core penetrates armor

Fragments of shell core and spall kill crew

HESH

Crew killed by spall and heat

Armor is pierced by shaped charge

HEAT

Crew killed by spall and high temperature jet of gas

Armor is pierced by shaped charge

APDS/APDSFS

Fragments of shell core and hot gasses kill crew

Armor is pierced by force of impact concentrated by hardened core

Parts of a Tank

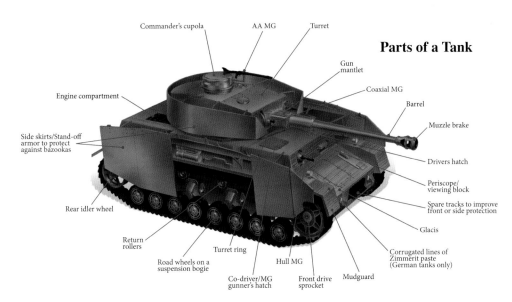

Commander's cupola — AA MG — Turret — Gun mantlet — Coaxial MG — Barrel — Muzzle brake — Engine compartment — Side skirts/Stand-off armor to protect against bazookas — Drivers hatch — Periscope/viewing block — Spare tracks to improve front or side protection — Glacis — Corrugated lines of Zimmerit paste (German tanks only) — Rear idler wheel — Return rollers — Road wheels on a suspension bogie — Turret ring — Co-driver/MG gunner's hatch — Hull MG — Front drive sprocket — Mudguard

of suspension involved springing the road wheels on a bogie against each other with a horizontally oriented volute spring.

IS eg IS-3—Iosif Stalin, a Russian heavy tank series named after "The Boss," Joseph Stalin.

Mk Mark, eg Churchill Mk VIII.

OQF Ordnance, quick firing. A gun that does not use separate loading ammunition; i.e., the propellant case and projectile are a single unit.

PzKpfw *Panzerkampfwagen* = tank/armored vehicle in German.

RCA *Régiment de Chasseurs d'Afrique*

RC *Régiment de Cuirasses*

SdKfz *Sonderkraftfahrzeug* = special-purpose motor vehicle in German.

SP Self-propelled.

s(SS)PzAbt *schwere (SS) Panzer Abteilung* = heavy Tank Battalion (usually Tigers). Some were SS, others German Army.

TD Tank destroyer—towed (antitank guns) or tracked (such as the M10 Wolverine).

VVSS Vertical volute spring suspension: this suspension involved mounting the road wheels to a bogie in pairs on arms and pivoting them against a vertically mounted volute spring, which was protected from damage by the bogie frame.

W As in M4A1(76)W. Wet ammunition stowage meant that main gun ammunition was stored in double-walled boxes between which was a mixture of water, antifreeze, and an anticorrosive agent to delay or eliminate ammunition fire if hit by an enemy shot.

Zimmerit Paste painted on German tanks to provide a surface that prohibited the application of anti-magnetic mines or sticky bombs.

Introduction

Right: *Collection of German tanks and equipment in a park outside Isigny. The Allies made use of captured vehicles but not to the same extent as the Germans did. The* Beutepanzer *included those taken from conquered nations—Czech, French, etc—and those captured in battle.* NARA

Opposite: *Understandably, as it was produced in such numbers, there are many Sherman survivors in Northwest Europe and museums around the world. This late war M4A1E8 HVSS is outside the National Museum of Military History in Diekirch, Luxembourg.*

Tanks are big lumps of metal. The small Panzer Is and IIs may have weighed less than 10 tons, but the armored behemoths such as the Jagdpanther or Tiger II weighed in at 45 and 70 tons respectively. For a scrap metal dealer they were certainly worth exploiting, and in the years after the end of the war most battlefield relics were cut up and melted down—those that weren't taken to be used as tractors by farmers, sold to other nations, employed by the military as range targets, or taken to exhibit in museums.

A few vehicles were preserved immediately in situ as reminders of acts of bravery, victories or simply the five years of war. At La Gleize, for example, locals paid the US Army to leave behind *Leibstandarte*'s Tiger II that currently sits outside the church and museum. At Houffalize, a Panther that had been blown into the river by a bomb blast was dragged into position on rue de Bastogne. Other locations used what influence they could to receive a tank: Leopoldsburg in Belgium, for example, where XXX Corps' CG, Gen Brian Horrocks, briefed his men on Operation Market Garden, pushed the Deputy Chief of the Belgian General Staff for a monument and received the M4A4 with a Firefly turret that stands outside the station today.

This book looks at these survivors, the stalwarts that endure all that the weather can throw at them and stand as silent guardians of the battlefields on which they or their compatriots fought with such distinction or nearby the tank museums of the world.

Often regarded as automotively challenged, in fact the Panther was rather more functional as shown by study of the war diary of the Hitlerjugend *Division—the 12th SS-Panzer Division. Between June 6 and July 11, 1944, the majority of the Panthers that were unserviceable were out of action mainly due to battle damage—including air attack as here—not mechanical failure. The major problem for the unit was that the repair and recovery assets within the battalion workshop platoon were unequal to the task asked of them. On top of this, the battalion itself received few replacement tanks.* NARA

By May 1940 the Germans had crossed the Meuse river near Sedan having taken the Low Countries by storm. The French counterattacked and elements of two battalions of Char B1s—around 34 tanks—engaged the Germans at Stonne on May 14. Capt Billotte in "Eure" knocked out two PzKpfw IVs and 11 PzKpfw III tanks as well as two PaK 36 anti-tank guns of 10th Panzer Division. Invulnerable to German guns, "Eure" took 140 hits without penetration. The battle raged one way with the village changing hands 17 times between May 15 and 17 and then the other before the Germans gained the upper hand. As a memorial after the war "Toulal" of 49e BCC was constructed from parts of several tanks. Les Meloures/WikiCommons

Below: *The monument at the Dukla Pass in Slovenia incorporates a PzKpfw IV and a T-34 locked in battle. After fighting in the area, KO'd tanks were left in situ to remember the events of fall 1944.*
Tom Timmermans

Opposite, Above: *PzKpfw IV Ausf H outside the Military Museum, Belgrade, Serbia.* Nataša Juhu Radovanović/WikiCommons (CC BY-SA 3.0

Opposite, Below: *Wirbelwind in the Base Borden Military Museum.* Balcer/WikiCommons (CC BY-SA 3.0)

Tank Museums of the World

Armored Warfare Museum, Poznań, Poland (reopening 2018).

Australian Armour and Artillery Museum in Cairns, Queensland, opened in 2014.

Base Borden Military Museum in Borden, Ontario, Canada, established in the 1990s.

Bovington Tank Museum in Dorset, England: quite simply the best, but we're biassed.

Canadian War Museum, in Ottawa, Ontario, whose new building opened in 2005.

Cavalry Tank Museum, Ahmednagar, Maharashtra, India, established 1994—the only museum of its kind in Asia.

General George Patton Museum of Leadership in Fort Knox, Kentucky.

German Tank Museum in Munster, Germany, opened in 1983.

Indian Cavalry Tank Museum, Maharashtra, India.

Kubinka Tank Museum, Moscow Oblast, Russia, opened 1972.

Military Museum, Belgrade, Serbia—open since the 19th century.

Military Technical Museum Lešany, Czech Republic, opened 1996.

Muckleburgh Collection, Weybourne, UK, opened in 1988.

Musée des Blindés, Saumur, France, opened in 1977.

Overloon War Museum, Netherlands, established 1946.

Parola Tank Museum, Finland, in 1961.

Royal Australian Armoured Corps Memorial and Army Tank Museum at Puckapunyal, opened 1970.

US Army Ordnance Training and Heritage Center (until 2010 the US Army Ordnance Museum at Aberdeen Proving Ground), Fort Lee, Petersburg, Virginia.

Wheatcroft Collection, Leicestershire, England, established in the 1980s.

Yad La-Shiryon, Israel, opened in the 1980s.

What was the best tank of the war?

The classic question is not so easily answered—although experts have, of course, had their say. One thing is certain: in northwest Europe in 1944 there was only one word on the lips of the Allies when attacked by German armor: Tiger! Every tank spotted was identified as a PzKpfw VI as is evidenced in so many photo captions from the period.

There's no doubt that if it were simply down to the fear factor the Tiger would win hands down. That fear was bred from the effectiveness of its gun, the famous 88, and the strength of its frontal armor against which so many Allied weapons acted merely as doorknockers. But the Tiger had flaws: automotively it was poor; it was too heavy to cross many European bridges; and it was built in too small numbers. The Allied tanks were able to swamp it.

The key to the answer is first to determine what a tank is for. American doctrine said that it wasn't to fight other tanks, but to target the rear of enemy positions as it exploited a breakout: making use of its mobility. The Germans went for heavy armor and a big gun.

All tanks have to balance the design elements of protection, gun, and mobility. To these three can be added three more yardsticks: durability, survivability, and flexibility. Durability, because a tank has to be able to take punishment and yet stay serviceable in the field; survivability, because the longer the crew survive, the better they become and the fewer easy pickings there are; and flexibility—the tank is a platform that can be upgunned or repurposed over a lifetime that is longer than a battle. Finally, tanks have to be affordable enough to be manufactured in sufficient quantities to ensure that the "best" doesn't mean the last one standing.

Let's examine three contenders: the American M4 Sherman, Russian T-34, and German Tiger.

Tank and SP Gun Production 1939–1945

Date	Canada	Germany	Hungary	Italy	Japan	UK	USA	USSR
1939	?	247	-	40	-	969	-	2,950
1940	?	1,643	-	250	315	1,399	331	2,794
1941	?	3,790	-	595	595	4,841	4,052	6,590
1942	?	6,180	)	1,252	557	8,611	24,997	24,446
1943	?	12,063	) 500	336	558	7,476	29,497	24,089
1944	?	19,002	)	-	353	4,600	17,565	28,963
1945	?	3,932	-	-	137	?	11,968	15,419
Total	5,678	46,857	500	2,473	2,515	27,896	88,410	105,251

Relative sizes of WWII AFVs.

PzKpfw II   T34/76   Churchill   M4 Sherman   PzKpfw IV Ausf E   Char B1 bis   PzKpfw VI Tiger   IS-III

German Tank Production 1939–1945

	Prewar	1939	1940	1941	1942	1943	1944	1945	Wartime	Total
PzKpfw I	1,893	-	-	-	-	-	-	-	-	1,893
PzKpfw II	1,223	15	99	265	848	803	151	-	2,181	3,404
PzKpfw 38(t)	78	153	367	678	652	1,008	2,356	1,335	6,549	6,627
PzKpfw III	98	157	1,054	2,213	2,958	3,379	4,752	1,136	15,649	15,747
PzKpfw IV	210	45	368	467	994	3,822	6,625	1,090	13,311	13,522
PzKpfw V Panther	-	-	-	-	-	1,849	4,003	705	6,557	6,557
PzKpfw VI E Tiger I	-	-	-	-	78	649	641	-	1,368	1,368
PzKpfw VI B Tiger II	-	-	-	-	-	1	428	140	569	569
Total	3,503	370	1,888	3,623	5,530	11,601	18,956	4,406	46,274	49,777

Tanks in Service 1939–1945

Canada

Ram	50 (Ram I)
	1094 (Ram II)
Grizzly	188

France

FCM 21	90
Renault R35	900
Renault D1/D2	260
Char B1 bis	300
Somua S35	400

Germany

See table on page 23.

Italy

L3	2,500
M11/39	100
M13/40	800

Japan

Type 95	?
Type 97 Chi-Ha	) 2,580
Type 97 Shinhoto/Chi-Ha	)

Poland

TKS	300
Vickers Mk E	38
7TPjw	95

United Kingdom

Challenger	200
Churchill	5,640
Comet (some postwar)	1,186
Cruiser I	125
Cruiser II	175
Cruiser III	65
Cruiser IV/IVA	855
Cruiser IV Covenanter	1,771
Cruiser VI Crusader (inc variants	5,300
Cruiser VII Cavalier	500
Cruiser VIII Centaur	950
Cruiser VIII Cromwell	4,016
Matilda I	140
Matilda II	2,987
Valentine (inc variants)	8,280**

United States

M3 Stuart	13,859
M5 Stuart	885*
M3 Lee/Grant	6,258
M4 (75mm) Sherman	33,403
M4 (76mm) Sherman	10,883
M4 (105mm) Sherman	4,680
M4 Sherman Firefly	2,100
M24 Chaffee	4,415
M26 Pershing	1,436

* also 1,420 built in Canada supplied to Russia
** 1,778 M8 HMCs built

USSR

BT-7	780
IS-2	3,854
IS-3	350
KV-1	3,010
KV-1S	1,232
T-60	c. 5,900
T-70	8,231
T-34	35,488
T-34/85	23,213

Right: *The business end of the Tiger. The Germans sacrificed mobility for a big gun and survivability. Tigers were able to pick off their opponents from long range—ranges at which their enemies' weapons were ineffective.*

Opposite: *German manufacturing couldn't turn out enough Tigers but it did make use of captured equipment. This is a Hetzer, a tank destroyer with a 75mm gun on a Czech Skoda-built PzKpfw 38(t) chassis. NARA*

Self-Propelled Guns 1939–1945

Designation	Gun	Chassis
Germany		
Hetzer	75mm PAK39	PzKpfw 38(t)
Marder II	75mm PAK40	PzKpfw II
Marder III	75mm PAK40	PzKpfw 38(t)
StuG IIIG	75mm StuK40	PzKpfw III
StuG IV	75mm StuK40	PzKpfw IV
PzKpfw IV/70 (V)	75mm StuK43	PzKpfw IV
Marder II	76.2mm StuK36(r)	PzKpfw II
Marder III	76.2mm PAK36(r)	PzKpfw 38(t)
Nashorn	88mm PAK43	PzKpfw IV
Jagdpanther	88mm PAK43	PzKpfw V
Ferdinand/Elefant	88mm PAK43	PzKpfw VI (I)
StuH42	105mm StuH42	PzKpfw III
Wespe	105mm le FH18	PzKpfw II
Jagdtiger	128mm PAK44	PzKpfw VI (II)
Grille	150mm sIG33	PzKpfw 38(t)
Hummel	150mm sFH18	PzKpfw IV

Designation	Gun	Chassis
Italy		
L40	47/32mm 35	L6/40
M40	75/18mm 35	M13/40
M41	75/18mm 35	M14/41
M42	75/18mm 35	M15/42
United Kingdom		
Bishop	25pdr	Valentine
Archer	17pdr	Valentine
Sexton	25pdr	M3 Ram
United States		
M3 75mm halftrack	75mm M1897A	M3 halftrack
M8 Scott	75mm M1A1	M5 Stuart
M18 Hellcat	76mm M1	-
M10 Wolverine	3 inch M7	M4
M36	90mm M3	M4
M4 (105mm)	105mm M2A1	M4
M7 Priest	105mm M2A1	M3
M7B1	105mm M2A1	M4
M12	155mm M1A1	M3
USSR		
SU-76M	76.2mm Zis-3	T-70M
SU-85	85mm D5S	T-34
SU-100	100mm D10S	T-34
SU-122	122mm M30S	T-34
SU-152	152mm ML20	KV-1S
ISU-122	122mm A195	IS-1
ISU-152	152mm ML20	IS-1

M4 Sherman

The M4 has had a bad press: "Ronson Lighter," "Tommy Cooker," the perjorative comments are well known. When set against the mighty Tiger, with its 88mm gun and 100mm of frontal armor, the Sherman seems to be second best. But appearances can be deceptive. In the hands of experts, the M4 proved to be more than effective. These comments come from the January 1946 *Military Review* by someone who really knew the score. Lt Col (later Brigadier General) Albin F. Irzyk "rode up front for Patton" as the commander of the 8th Tank Battalion of Third Army's 4th Armored Division. He said:

"The German 88 is more powerful than any American tank gun used during the course of the war. The German tank is much heavier and therefore its armor is much thicker than that of any American tank. The tracks of the former are much wider, with perhaps a less vulnerable suspension system than that of the latter. If I stop here, as I am convinced so many have, there is no question but that the German tank is a much better one than our own. In this paragraph there is material, indeed, for sensational headlines in newspapers in the States

Today, however, let us not stop here. Let us go on! What is the fuel capacity of the German Tiger tank? How long and how far is it able to run on a tank full of gasoline? Does it burn much oil? What is the composition and life of its tracks? How many rounds of ammunition is it able to stow? What is the life (discounting its being hit in action) of a Tiger tank? Is its engine comparatively free of maintenance problems? If maintenance problems occur, are they easy to remedy? How long and how much skill is required to change an engine? Is the German tank able to move for long distances and continuous periods at a steady rate of speed? How is its endurance? Could fifty-three Tiger tanks, for instance, move from the vicinity of Fenetrange, France, in the Saar, to an area near Bastogne, Belgium, a distance of 151 miles, in less than twenty-four hours to answer a fire call as did tanks of the Fourth Armored Division? ... Could the German tank roll for several hours at a speed of twenty-five miles per hour in exploiting a breakthrough?"

Irzyk goes on to discuss the time that the M4 suffered most: in the quagmire of the European fall in 1944, when mobility meant little and the "lumbering, heavy, mobile pillbox" —the Tiger—enjoyed the advantages of short supply lines, and the defender's choice of terrain allowed them to make the best of their guns' longer range and hitting ability.

However, at this stage of the war, along came the improved M4A3E8 with its improved engine, improved suspension,

and 76mm gun with better armor-piercing ammunition. Irzyk considered that version the most effective as was proved in the last months of the war. He pointed to the mechanical reliability; the speed of engine change; the range. M4s could cross those bridges the heavier German tanks couldn't (a major problem for *Leibstandarte* in the Ardennes); they could be towed when disabled; their armor didn't shatter; they had power traverse. All-in-all, "I believe that even the most prejudiced or the most difficult to convince will nod toward the Sherman."

Irzyk didn't mention the Firefly, the British upgunning of the M4 with a 17pdr. Available for D-Day, Fireflies contributed much to Allied success in Normandy, capable of knocking out Tigers and Panthers at long range. Initially there was only one Firefly available for each troop, but this ratio improved as the war proceeded. In total around 2,150 Fireflies were produced.

M4 Production by Type

Type	Number Produced	Production Dates	Manufacturers
Prototype	1	September 1941	Aberdeen Proving Ground
M4 (75) (incl. composites)	6,748	July 1942–January 1944	Pressed Steel Car, ALCO, Baldwin LW, Pullman Std, Chrysler
M4A1(75)	6,281	February 1942–December 1943	Lima LW, Pressed Steel Car, Pacific Car & Foundry
M4A2(75)	8,053	April 1942–May 1944	Pullman Std, ALCO, Baldwin LW, Fisher, Federal Machine & Welder
M4A3(75)	1,690	June 1942–September 1943	Ford
M4A4	7,499	July 1942–November 1943	Chrysler
M4A6	75	October 1943–February 1944	Chrysler
M4(105)	800	February 1944–September 1944	Chrysler
M4 (105) HVSS	841	September 1944–March 1945	Chrysler
M4A1(76)W	2,171	January 1944–December 1944	Pressed Steel Car
M4A1(76) HVSS	1,255	January 1945–July 1945	Pressed Steel Car
M4A2(76)W	1,594	May 1944–December 1944	Fisher
M4A2(76) HVSS	1,321	January 1945–May 1945	Fisher, Pressed Steel Car
M4A3(75)W	3,071	February 1944–March 1945	Fisher
M4A3E2 Jumbo	254	Jun 1944– July 1944	Fisher
M4A3(76)W	1,925	March 1944–December 1944	Fisher, Chrysler
M4A3(76) HVSS	2,617	August 1944–April 1945	Chrysler
M4A3(105)	500	May 1944–September 1944	Chrysler
M4A3(105) HVSS	2,539	September 1944–June 1945	Chrysler
TOTAL	49,234	February 1942–July 1945	

M4 and Variants Production by Year

	Total	1942	1943	1944	1945
M4 series, 75mm gun	33,671	8,017	21,245	3,758	651
M4 series, 76mm gun	10,883	0	0	7,135	3,748
M4 series, 105mm howitzer	4,680	0	0	2,286	2,394
M10 and M36 Tank Destroyer	6,706	639	6,067	0	0
M36B1 Tank Destroyer (on M4A3 hull and chassis)	187	0	0	187	0
M7 Priest	3,490	2,028	786	500	176
M7B1 Priest	826	0	0	664	162
M12 (155mm gun)	100	60	40	0	0
M30 cargo carrier for M12	100	60	40	0	0
M40 (155mm gun)	418	0	0	0	418
M43 (8-inch howitzer)	24	0	0	0	24
M32 Tank Recovery Vehicle	1,599	0	31	1,050	498
Special purpose tanks on M4 chassis *	497	0	355	142	0
TOTAL	63,181	10,804	28,564	15,722	8,071

M4 Production by Manufacturer

Manufacturer	Number Produced	Types
Aberdeen PG	1	Prototype
Federal Machine & Welder	540	M4A2(75)
Pacific Car & Foundry	926	M4A1(75)
Baldwin LW	1245	M4(75), M4A2(75)
Lima Locomotive Works	1655	M4A1(75)
Ford	1690	M4A3(75)
American Loco	2300	M4(75), M4A2(75)
Pullman Standard	3426	M4(75), M4A2(75)
Pressed Steel Car	8147	M4(75), M4A1(75), M4A1(76)W, M4A2(76)W
Fisher	11358	M4A2(75), M4A2(75)D, M4A3(75)W, M4A2(76)W, M4A3(76)W, M4A3E2
Chrysler	17947	M4A4(75), M4 composite, M4A6, M4A3(76)W, M4A3(105), M4(105)
TOTAL	49234	

T-34

Just as the M4 seems to attract criticism, so the T-34 is almost always named the best tank of the war, mainly because of its balance between mobility—great automotive reliability—protection in the form of sloping armor, and a good gun. Its range wasn't brilliant, but extra fuel could be carried in drums—although that had its bad points as this account shows:

"By chance our regiment met on the second day of the Russian war the first regiment of T-34s that had been in the Russian Army; and we, of course, had no knowledge at all of this tank; and, in the first phase of this battle, my tank was shot; and my driver was killed. Four tanks were in our group, and they all suffered the same fate. The commander's cupola had been shot away, and two officers and two sergeants were dead. We had further fighting in the morning and in the afternoon, and then we finally burned some of these tanks by using 76mm high explosive shells with delay fuses (one-fourth second).

So because they had all tanks with fuel on the rear we could make them burn."

In fact, closer examination of the T-34 shows that it had a number of defects which led to many problems on the battlefield. First, its fire control was poor. This was partly down to crew tasking: in the small two-man turret the tank's commander was also the gun aimer and firer and could also have other command requirements (eg platoon leader). Limited gun depression, extremely poor vision aids, and main gun optics didn't help. The commander didn't have a cupola but one periscope with poor glass; radios were few and far between which meant little or no tactical control on the battlefield. And if the commander tried to ride with his head out of the turret ... his hatch opened forward blocking his sightlines. Ammunition was scarce. When one adds inexperienced, badly trained crews—most of the Russian crews had but a few days' experience in the tank—then it isn't surprising to see that Operation Barbarossa led to T-34 losses of around five for each German tank knocked out. This would improve, though, as the war progressed and crews survived combat and gained experience, but it is still a staggering figure. However, one thing did shine through: the T-34's armor was more than a match for the Germans' anti-tank guns of the time—until there were sufficient 88s to go round, the 37mm antitank guns were ineffective, and the PzKpfw IV's short-barreled 75mm shells bounced off.

Further examination of the statistics show that T-34s were being killed by tanks that had been identified as its inferior: so 60 percent of the 6,600 T-34s lost June 1941–September 1942 were to German tanks with 50mm guns: the PzKpfw IIIJ with

its KwK39 gun was introduced in spring 1942 as was the IVF with its KwK40 75mm. 1943 saw the introduction of the Tiger (in January) and the Panther (summer), the frontal armor of both being impervious to the T-34's 76.2mm gun.

German tactics and training also clearly helped, but as the war went on and the German advantages were eroded as the top crews died, the T-34s were still knocked out in high numbers. In 1943, some 14,700 T-34s were lost, and this finally led to design improvements—the T-34/76 was replaced by the T-34/85 which had a new three-man turret mounting the improved 85mm M1944 ZIS-S53 L/51.5 gun. Crew training also improved and by 1944, the Russian tank arm was a force to be reckoned with.

It mustn't be assumed that the fighting during this period went all the Germans' way. In winter 1941 the 1st Guards Armored Brigade proved the effectiveness of the T-34 against anything the Germans could throw at it if it were manned by halfway decent crews. Then came the great tank battle of Kursk starting on July 5, 1943. On July 13, II SS-Panzer Corps attacked towards Prokhorovka and was met by the 5th Guards Tank Army. Each side lost around 300 tanks, but the Russians had gained a major victory. By blunting the cream of the Waffen-SS, the Russians had turned the tide of the war on the Eastern Front. From now on, the Germans would be on the defensive.

This didn't stop the Germans knocking out 23,700 AFVs in 1944 of which 58 percent were T-34s and many the new model. In total, the Soviets lost upward of 44,000 T-34s during the war, 82 percent of its production. Lack of suitable recovery vehicles meant that—especially in the early years—vehicles that could have been recovered were lost, but losses on this scale show that there was more wrong than simply the crew. It's hard to suggest that the T-34 was the best tank in the world with these figures.

T-34 and Variants Production by Type

Type	1939	1940	1941	1942	1943	1944	1945	Total
Tanks								
T-28	131	13						144
T-34		115	3016	12,661	15,710	3,986		35,488
T-34/85						10,662	12,551	23,213
T-44							25	545
SP guns								
SU-76				25	1,908	7,155	2,966	12,054
SU-85				761	1,578	315		2,654
SU-100						500	1,060	1,560
SU-122				26	612			638
TOTAL	131	128	3,016	13,473	19,808	22,618	16,606	76,296

Opposite: *T-34/85 in Berlin. Note the size of the new turret and altered gun mantle.*

Below: *Now this really is "Mission Accomplished"! The Red Army occupies Berlin and this T-34/85 has the Brandenburg Gate as a backdrop. Note the bedsprings welded to the sides to act as stand-off armor to protect against Panzerfausts and Panzerschrecks.*
Both: George Forty Collection

Tiger

Below: *The massive armor and mantle of the Tiger. On the right, the hole is for the Turmzielfernrohr 9c monocular sight introduced in April 1944. On the left, the hole is for the 7.92mm MG34 coaxial MG.*

Opposite: *The Sturmtiger was a 68-ton beast. An assault gun that made use of the Tiger I chassis, it mounted an immense 380mm RW61 rocket launcher. 18 were built.* Both: George Forty Collection

Reading Allied accounts of the battle of Normandy it seems that there were Tigers around every corner. Just as Germans on the Eastern Front reported every Russian tank as a T-34—partly out of respect—so every German tank in Normandy was a Tiger, and therefore invulnerable to Allied tank shot and with a main armament that could slice through Allied vehicles at will. In fact, there were fewer than 150 Tiger Is and IIs in Normandy in the hands of one army (503) and two schwere SS-Panzer Abteilungen (SS heavy tank battalions) 101 and 102—and possibly a few with Panzer Lehr. *Sledgehammers* analyzes the combat effectiveness of these battalions. They destroyed some 510 Allied tanks, but other than a few Tigers shipped back to

Germany, every one of the Tigers was lost, 132 while committed to or retreating from Normandy, around 48 to direct ground combat (although 10 remain unaccounted for). Five were lost at Villers-Bocage in the aftermath of Wittmann's assault on British 7th Armoured Division. On the Eastern Front, the Tiger debuted in August 1942 and over the two years to August 1944 lost 749 vehicles. Against that, *Sledgehammers* assesses the Tigers' kill ratio at around 12.2: 1 in combat; 5.4: 1 against all losses—although the latter does include the final losses when retreating.

There can be no doubt, however, that the Tiger was the best-protected, best-armed most-feared AFV on the battlefield. Its protection meant that their crews survived for longer and became more experienced. The 88mm main gun's killing power was second to none—but while they had a significant effect on whichever battlefield they fought, they were used to shore up the Germans' defenses and could not deliver the decisive offensive blow for which they were designed.

Mechanically, the Tiger was unreliable. It broke down too easily. This gave low operational rates and, because of its weight and lack of a decent ARV, low recovery rates—and this led to a correspondingly high destruction by crew figure (41% of those lost). The high weight—Tiger I was 62.8 US short tons (57,000kg) and Tiger II, 76.9 tons (69,800kg)— also contributed to its poor range and inability to bridge Europe's many streams and small rivers whose crossings were just not up to it.

It was, however, an effective tank killer—without doubt the best of the three tanks featured here. The Tiger may have

Tiger I and II kills and losses

Unit	Tiger losses Total (in action)	Enemy losses
sPzAbt 501	120 (24)	450
sPzAbt 502	107 (88)	1,400
sPzAbt 503	252 (113)	1,700*
sPzAbt 504	109 (29)	250
sPzAbt 505	126 (47)	900
sPzAbt 506	179 (61)	400
sPzAbt 507	104 (43)	600
sPzAbt 508	78 (15)	100
sPzAbt 509	120 (76)	500
sPzAbt 510	65 (35)	200
sSS-PzAbt 101	107 (72)	500
sSS-PzAbt 102	76 (38)	600
sSS-PzAbt 103	39 (10)	500
III/PzRegt Grossdeutschland	98 (62)	500
TOTAL	1,580 (713—45%)	8,600

* Almost certainly overstated

Tiger production

	1942	1943	1944	1945	Total
Tiger I	78	649	623	-	1,350
Sturmtiger	-	-	18	-	18
Tiger II	-	1	377	112	490
Jagdtiger	-	-	51	28	79
TOTAL	78	650	1,069	140	1,937

been unreliable automotively, but it was also extremely survivable with heavy armor protection that shielded its crew in battle. Old crews are wise crews, and the battle-savvy veterans of the German heavy tank battalions proved this on eastern and and western fronts.

Opposite, Above: *The* Tigerfibel *(operating manual) was for platoon leaders (*Zugführer*) and Tiger people (*leute*).* Marseille77-the-blueprints.com/WikiCommons

Opposite, Below and Below: *Tigers were certainly not invulnerable, but of the 1,580 lost, 55 percent were not combat casualties.* George Forty Collection

Chapter 1: D-Day

Although the Dieppe Raid, which took place on August 19, 1942, was an expensive disaster, it taught the Allies many lessons—such as trying to capture a heavily defended port was likely to fail and that specialist vehicles would be necessary to help attacking forces land and negotiate the difficult coastal terrain of sand, shingle, and dune as well the German strongpoints, obstacles and anti-tank defenses that made up Hitler's Atlantic Wall. In early 1943 the British 79th Armoured Division, under the command of Maj Gen Percy Hobart, was given the responsibility of developing specialized vehicles and tactics to support the Allied troops in what became known as the D-Day landings of June 6, 1944. The distinctive and unusual vehicles that were produced became known as "Hobart's Funnies" and the 79th, rather than operating as a single division, was distributed in smaller units across other the Allied divisions taking part in the beach landings and subsequent operations. The vehicles themselves were made by modifying existing AFVs—primarily Sherman, Churchill and Grant tanks. The Sherman Duplex Drive was an amphibious swimming tank that was used on all five beaches during D-Day, whereas the Sherman Crab was a mine flail. The Churchill was also fitted with either an anti-mine flail, a flamethrower (the Crocodile) or modified to become the Armoured Vehicle Royal Engineers (AVRE). AVREs came in a number of forms including with a mine plough, a spigot mortar, fascines, a bobbin carpet layer (for tanks to drive over soft sand) or a bridgelayer (ARK Armoured Ramp Carrier). The CDL (Canal Defence Light) was a Grant fitted with a searchlight in its turret, to provide light during night operations or temporarily blind enemy forces. Although there were problems—primarily in the lack of training time—and, therefore, confidence in these vehicles, they soon proved their worth in the assault phase of the invasion and continued to be invaluable afterwards in the progress across Europe to the German homeland.

Location: Slapton Sands,
Devon, UK
Commemorating:
Exercise Tiger disaster
Combatants: US Navy;
Royal Navy; German Navy
Date: April 27, 1944

Right and Opposite: *This
Sherman DD was recovered
from the seabed where it
had lain since the attack by
German E-boats on Exercise
Tiger—one of the pre-invasion
exercises held in England in
spring 1944. Its recovery on
May 19, 1984, was researched,
organized, and financed by
Ken Small, who wanted to
remember those lost at Slapton
Sands.* Cowbridgeguide.co.uk/
WikiCommons (CC BY 3.0)

M4A1(75) Sherman DD Medium Tank

This tank is an original from the 1944 Exercise Tiger and
has a very tragic back story, but also a redemptive end in the
actions of a single local man, Neil Small, whose dedication
ensured its retrieval from the sea and subsequent revival in
1984 as a memorial to the casualties of that fateful day. The
live-fire beach landings practiced by US forces at Slapton
Sands were carried out in preparation for the D-Day landings
on Utah Beach. A series of awful errors and bad luck killed
many more US soldiers than died later on that beach in
Normandy. On April 27, 1944, nine large tank landing ships
(LSTs) with 30,000 troops and armor aboard, enacted a
dawn landing on Slapton Beach, Devon accompanied by a
live naval bombardment which was supposed to precede it.
Delays to the schedule along with confused communications
resulted in the first deaths amongst the landing forces to
"friendly fire" from their own fleet. One of the two Royal
Navy corvettes assigned to protect the exercise then collided
with an LST and had to return to port for repairs. The other
was leading the convoy of eight LSTs across Lyme Bay
when they were spotted and attacked by nine German fast
attack boats armed with torpedoes in a lightning raid from
their base across the Channel at Cherbourg. In a matter of
minutes two LSTs were sunk and another set on fire, while a
fourth was hit once again by "friendly fire." Still more deaths
occurred when the troops in full kit put on their life jackets
around their waists—for they were then turned upside down
and drowned. With D-Day imminent, the whole calamitous
event was officially denied and survivors sworn to secrecy.
Somewhere between 650 and 900 died men during Exercise
Tiger, while only 200 were killed later on Utah.

Right: *Cromwell IV in Nijmegen during Operation Garden. The Cromwell was extremely automotively reliable but had a rotten tank gun—the Ordnance QF 75mm, produced by boring out the 6pdr 57mm AT gun to 75mm. This worked well when it employed an HE shell against infantry, but the anti-tank round wasn't good.* via Tim Pruyn

Opposite: *7th Armoured Division memorial at Thetford. The division was not happy about giving up their Shermans: events at Villers-Bocage underlined the reality of their misgivings.* Leo Marriott

Mk VIII (A27M) Cromwell Mk IV Cruiser Tank

Sited at what used to be the entrance to a busy WWII army camp, now part of the Thetford Forest Park, is a Cromwell Mk IV commemorating all who served in the Desert Rats —an almost mythic formation of the British Army that gave Britain its first victories against the Italians and then the Germans in North Africa. The only time this division was in the UK between 1940 and the end of the war was for five months at Thetford Camp, Norfolk to refit in preparation for the 1944 D-Day landings. 7th Armoured saw action in North Africa, Italy, France, Belgium, Holland, and Germany.

The memorial is the result of a special effort made by one particular old Desert Rat, Les Dinning, who realized that people walking round the park knew nothing of its military past and so began a successful funding campaign in 1996. Construction started in July 1998 and the memorial was inaugurated on October 23, 1998, by Field Marshal Lord Carver, who fought in North Africa with the division. The tank has been restored as a replica of Gunner Dinning's "5 Able" of B Squadron, 1 RTR, which bore the inscription "Little Audrey Laughed and Laughed" and so was also known as "Audrey."

7th Armoured Division was equipped mainly with the new Cromwell tanks while stationed in Thetford between January and May 1944, and was the first formation to take the tank into action when they sailed from Felixstowe on June 5, 1944, the first tanks landing on Gold Beach on the evening of D-Day. Later, in a bazooka attack on September 26, 1944, tank commander Sgt A. Davies and wireless operator Cpl "Taffy" Glenton were both killed and were subsequently buried in Holland. On June 27, 2004, an additional plaque commemorating the Desert Rats of the 4th and 7th Armoured Brigades from 1945 to 2003 was added.

Right: *The identity of this
AVRE, "T68024/B Bulldog,"
was used when repainting the
AVRE that stood as a 3rd
Division memorial near the
Sword Beach seafront at
Hermanville. After having
resided in Normandy from
1987 to 2000, "Bulldog" returned to Duxford for display
in IWM where it can be seen
now. Here it is passed by Universal carriers of
3rd Division's MG battalion,
2nd Middlesex Regiment.*
George Forty Collection

Opposite: *"One Charlie"
after its 2009 repainting.*
Richard Wood

Churchill Mk IV AVRE

Just inland from the beach at Graye-sur-Mer where it had foundered into a flooded crater and been abandoned on June 6, 1944 during Operation Overlord, sits the Churchill Mk IV AVRE "One Charlie." All six members of the crew escaped but immediately afterwards came under heavy mortar fire, with all but two consequently killed. It bears the bull's head flash of 26 Assault Squadron, Royal Engineers who were attached to the 7th Canadian Infantry Brigade for the landings on Juno Beach.

The AVREs were one of Gen Percy Hobart's "Funnies"— tanks that were modified with a variety of weapons and tools expressly for the purpose of helping the Allied forces get ashore, punch through the enemy's defenses, and establish a critical bridgehead. AVREs could be equipped with fascines, flails, Bangalore torpedoes, and bridges. This one was armed with 290mm Petard Spigot Mortar replacing the main gun, which fired an ungainly cylindrical projectile—nicknamed the "flying dustbin"—armed with a 28lb high explosive warhead to a range of approximately 300ft at a low velocity. It was used for breaching pillboxes, bunkers, and other concrete fortifications. "One Charlie" lay buried on the beach where it had foundered for 32 years until its recovery and restoration in 1976 at the French Army workshops in Caen, and was unveiled at its present location on October 15, 1977. During its salvage it was visited by the two surviving members of its original crew.

"One Charlie" was repainted in 2009 by 26th Armoured Engineer Squadron, 32nd Engineer Regiment—the direct descendants of the assault squadron on Juno beach in 1944.

Mk VIII (A27L) Centaur IV "Seawolf" CS Tank

Above Right: *"Hunter," from H Troop, 2 Battery, 1 RM Armoured Support Regt, which supported the attack on Christot on June 16.* George Forty Collection

Below Right: *Detail of the turret of "Seawolf," showing the degree markings that allowed an external artillery officer to ensure the correct firing line.* Richard Wood

Opposite: *"Seawolf" used to stand opposite the Cafe Gondrée at Pegasus Bridge before moving to its current home in Hermanville.* Leo Marriott

A confusion arises at this site from the plaque referring to a Churchill Mk III AVRE tank which previously stood here, however the AFV now resident is an A27L Cruiser Mk VIII Centaur IV CS (Close Support) tank with the name "Seawolf." It is, in fact, a composite assembled at the Imperial War Museum, Duxford, UK by marrying an original Centaur Dozer chassis with a Cavalier turret—both tanks being based on the Crusader. However it is symbolic of similar vehicles that were known as Hobart's "Funnies" and as part of the Royal Marines Armoured Support Group were critical to the success of the D-Day landings which took place at Sword Beach.

Various Centaurs were modified in preparation for the event, including 114 Centaur Mk IVs, which were armed with a 95mm (3.74 in) howitzer along with 51 HE rounds and fitted with wading gear over engine inlet valves and gun covers to enable a beach landing. Because of its low silhouette the Centaur CS could also be fired "blind"—while hidden from view inside the landing craft. It is for this reason that "Seawolf" has distinctive compass point markers around its turret—the 360° north marker painted at the rear and the 180° marker indicating south at the front. An outside spotter would call in the target using degrees and distance and the gunner would fire blind over the boat's front exit ramp, targeting enemy strongpoints, gun emplacements, and fortifications. Unfortunately, the pitching of the landing craft meant that accurate shooting wasn't possible.

CS Centaurs served from the June 1944 landings through Europe until the final VE-Day in May 1945.

M4A4(75) Sherman DD "Bold" Medium Tank

Right: *The metal frame necessary to attach the canvas around the DD Shermans is obvious on the example at Courseulles.*

Opposite, Inset: *"Bold," commanded by Major Stuart Duncan, was swamped 200 yards from the beach and lay there until 1970 when it was recovered.*

Opposite: *"Bold" has a number of plaques on its side, remembering Canadian units that landed over Juno Beach.*

This Sherman DD, as the memorial dedicated by the First Hussars to the memory of all who participated in this operation explains, is an original from the battle that was recovered 27 years after foundering and sinking in unexpectedly heavy seas on its way to the Juno Beach. At 07:30hrs on June 6, 1944, the Sherman DDs of 6th Canadian Armoured Regiment (First Hussars) in support of the 7th Canadian Infantry Brigade of the 3rd Infantry Division assaulted and overpowered enemy defenses between Courseulles-sur-Mer and Bernières-sur-Mer.

These tanks used the Straussler flotation system to make Sherman M4s seaworthy in good conditions and so provide armor to support the troops going ashore. A canvas and metal frame was fixed around the edge of the hull above the tracks. It reached above the turret, and was then held rigid by inflating 36 rubber tubes embedded within it with compressed air. This provided the tank with enough buoyancy to float. The exhaust pipe was raised and the underside waterproofed. Propulsion was provided with the addition of two propellers powered by the tank's rear track idler wheels. This dual method of using the tracks on land and in water gave the system its name of Duplex Drive. Unfortunately, due to the weather conditions on June 6, many Sherman DDs—particularly those on Omaha Beach—were swamped by heavy seas, but enough made it ashore to make a difference in the hard-fought battle to secure the bridgehead.

The Canadians took Courseulles by 10:00 and behind a line of old ships deliberately sunk to provide a breakwater, its tiny port was quickly repaired. As early as June 8, it was used to bring in reinforcements and equipment. Across the road close by the Sherman, a German KwK 39 AT gun with its shield sporting direct hits also commemorates the battle.

JUNO BEACH

At 0730 hours 6th June 1944, the 6th Canadian Armoured Regiment (First Hussars) in support of the 7 Canadian Infantry Brigade of the 3 Canadian Infantry Division, assaulted and overpowered enemy defences between Courseulles-sur-Mer and Bernieres-sur-Mer. This tank, recovered from the sea nearly 27 years after launching, is dedicated by the First Hussars, to the memory of all who participated in this operation.

DUPLEX DRIVE (DD) TANK

The Duplex Drive Sherman Tank had a waterproof chassis fitted with a collapsible canvas screen and rubber tubes inflated with air. It was moved through the water by two propellors at the rear, and on reaching shore reverted to a normal tank.

M4A1E8(76) HVSS Sherman Medium Tank

M4A1E8(76) HVSS SHERMAN

Location: Utah Beach Museum, 50480 Sainte-Marie-du-Mont, France
Commemorating: Operation Overlord D-Day landings on Utah Beach
Combatants: US Army; German Army
Date: June 6, 1944

Right: *US 3rd Armored Division, December 1944, in the Ardennes. On the left an M4A1(76)W and on the right a "Jumbo," an M4A3E2 with extra armor on turret, glacis, and transmission housing.* NARA

Opposite: *The later production M4A1s were made by Pressed Steel, armed with the improved M1A1C 76mm gun, and had a different suspension system.*

This M4 tank sits outside the Musée du Débarquement at Utah Beach—a museum situated directly above the beach where the first American troops landed on the Cotentin Peninsula on June 6. Founded in 1962 by the mayor of Sainte-Marie-du-Mont to tell the story of the US landings, it incorporated one of the German command bunkers of strongpoint WN5. Major expansions in 1994 and 2011 produced a premier museum with a rich collection of objects, vehicles, materials, digital and oral histories, including a B-26 Marauder bomber and the only known surviving LCVP (Landing Craft Vehicle Personnel) to have taken part on D-Day.

However, the current Sherman outside the museum is certainly not one that took part in the invasion. In fact, it is an M4A1(76) HVSS model, one of the last WWII variants of the Sherman, which arrived in Europe in December 1944 just in time for the Battle of the Bulge. It was armed with a long-barreled high velocity 76mm M1 main gun and two Browning M1919A4 machine guns, one in a frontal ball mount on the hull and the other mounted coaxially with the main gun in the turret. The E8 was also fitted with new horizontal volute spring suspension and had wider 23-inch tracks than the usual 16 inches, improving its stability and cross-country performance.

Despite being pushed a kilometer off course by strong currents, the American landings on Utah (primarily US 4th Infantry Division and 70th Tank Battalion in four separate waves) went smoothly, with the tanks launched much closer to the shore and all but a few reaching the beach successfully—unlike Omaha where most were inundated by the high seas.

US Shermans Around Omaha

Location: M4A4T: Outside the Musée Memorial d'Omaha Beach, Saint-Laurent-sur-mer
M4A1(76)W: Outside the Overlord Museum, Colleville-sur-Mer
Commemorating: Operation Overlord D-Day landings on Omaha Beach
Combatants: US Army; German Army
Date: June 6, 1944

Right: *The M4A1 outside the Overlord Museum carries the markings for First Army's 741st Tank Battalion.*

Opposite: *M4A4T outside the Musée Memorial d'Omaha Beach. Note the three-piece bolted hull and M34A1 gun mantle. The M4A4 was lengthened to take the Chrysler WC Multibank engine with a top speed of 25mph. 7,499 M4A4s were built.*

M4A4T: This Sherman M4A4T sits outside the Musée Memorial d'Omaha Beach, somewhat the worse for wear and needing a coat of paint and some TLC. It was armed with a 75mm M3 main gun and had three Browning machine guns—two .30cal M1919A and a single .50cal affixed to the top of the turret. The letter "T" at the end identifies the tank as having been upgraded by the French Army after WWII with a new engine, air filters, and extra armor-plating welded to the front and back of the hull and on the top of the turret.

M4A1(76)W: Side-by-side on the front lawn outside the Overlord Museum are an M10 Wolverine tank destroyer and a M4A1 Sherman. The M4A1 had the same engine and armament as the M4 but the key difference was that its upper hull was made from a single huge casting, which was state of the art technology at the time. This version was produced longer than any other hull type and it also took all the upgrades including a larger hull hatch, the T23 turret with 76mm gun, and HVSS suspension system.

The Sherman DD landings on Omaha were cursed with high winds, strong currents, and rough seas and the tanks were released too far out. Of the 32 launched by US 741st Tank Battalion only five reached the beach: the rest were overwhelmed by the waves and sank. However, realizing the situation the next 32 Shermans of US 743rd Tank Battalion stayed in their LCT landing craft and landed directly onto the beach, where they were able to give crucial support in securing the American bridgehead.

M10 Wolverine Gun Motor Carriage

M10 WOLVERINE

Location: Outside the Musée Overlord, Colleville-sur-Mer
Commemorating: Operation Overlord D-Day landings on Omaha Beach
Combatants: US Army; German Army
Date: June 6, 1944

Right: *M10 tank destroyer. The US fielded 52 TD battalions in Europe.* George Forty Collection

Opposite: *The excellent Overlord Museum was opened in 2013. It's based on the collection of the late Michael Leloup. The M10 TD out front carries the markings of 703rd TD Battalion of Third Army.*

This US M10 tank destroyer sits alongside the M4A1(76)W Sherman outside the Musée Overlord at Colleville-sur-Mer. The M10 was the most produced US tank destroyer of WWII and was in use right up to its end, although latterly both the more modern M16 and M36 were introduced. The M10 was based on an M4 chassis with an open-topped turret mounting a 3in (76.2mm) M7 gun firing HE and AP rounds. There was also .50cal Browning machine gun. It had a crew of five (commander, driver, and three gun crew) and was powered by a General Motors 6046 diesel engine with a top road speed of 32 mph and an operational range of 186 miles.

When first used in the Tunisian desert in 1943 the M10s could handle any German tanks that came their way, and with their speed they were highly maneuverable and liked by their crews for the ease of observation and escapability. However, by late 1944 the M10's disadvantages had become more apparent. They were too thinly armored and the open turret left the turret crew highly vulnerable to shrapnel as evinced by their attrition rate in the battle for Europe. Armored tops were improvised in an attempt to cope with threats from urban, bocage, and forest environments where snipers, grenades, Panzerschreck, and Panzerfaust teams began to take their toll. The M10's firepower now had little effect on the armor of the latest more heavily armored Panthers and Tigers unless up very close and the hand-operated turret took two minutes to fully traverse.

The M10 was supplied to various Allied armies including the British and the Free French. The British called it the Wolverine and later modified it, adding a heavier 17pdr gun which made it a more potent tank destroyer—the 17pdr SP Achilles.

Sexton Mk II Self-Propelled Gun

SEXTON Mk II

Location: Avenue du 6 Juin, 14114 Ver-sur-Mer, Normandy, France
Commemorating: Operation Overlord D-Day landings on Gold Beach
Combatants: British Army; German Army
Date: June 6, 1944

Right: *Porpoise ammo carrier.*

Opposite: *Positioned at the rear of the attacking forces on King Sector of Gold Beach, 86th Field Regiment Sextons fired on the beach at La Rivière for some time before being called to land at 08:30. They immediately had inland fire missions. The markings identify:*
• *28 = bridge classification*
• *1147 = unit (86th Field Regt) serial number*
• *shield = BR Second Army*
• *AA = A gun of A Troop; the red square indicates senior battery*

This Sexton II sits in the town of Ver-sur-Mer, in the middle of the memorial square called Espace Robert Kiln—in honor of Major Robert Kiln who served in the 86th Field Regiment, which landed on Gold Beach. It was donated by his son who knew that his father's regiment was the only one to land and use Sextons on D-Day.

The Sexton was a British version of the M7 Priest 105mm SP gun that had been provided originally by the US, but with which they had operational problems—mainly because the gun was not of a caliber used by Britain and required unique ammunition. Instead the British had their own version made using first a Canadian Ram chassis, and then—with the Sexton II—using the chassis of the Canadian version of the Sherman M4: the Grizzly. The Sexton mounted a British Ordnance QF 25pdr Mk II howitzer that had full elevation, a traverse of 25° left and 15° right with a range of 36,600ft. It was intended for indirect fire support directed by forward observers. It also had two light Bren guns for self-defense. The six-man crew of driver, commander, radio-operator and the three-man gun crew all rode in the fighting compartment. The 86th (Hertfordshire Yeomanry) Field Regiment, RA began using their guns while still in their landing craft, continuing on the beach directed by forward observers far ahead with the advancing infantry.

Just next to the Sexton is a unique survival from the landings: a Porpoise Ammunition Carrier Mk 1 No 2 (the larger version), used by both tanks and SP guns to carry extra ammunition behind them for first replenishment in the early stages of a beach assault. They were called Porpoises because they were waterproof and designed to be pulled while submerged using two tow-bars fitted with an explosive quick-release mechanism. Once on the beach, the sledge was dragged to a collection point to provided an instant ammunition reserve. Although a good idea, in practice they had a limited success and were considered more trouble than they were worth by most tank crews.

M5A1 Stuart Light Tank

The M5 light tank, named the Stuart by the British, was a development of the earlier M3 with twin Cadillac engines giving a maximum speed of 36mph. With a crew of four and a 37mm M6 main gun it entered service in 1942. It was replaced in 1944 by the superior M24 Chaffee. The M5 first saw action in North Africa and most US tank battalions had a company of light tanks, although latterly its function was limited to infantry fire support roles.

The M5A1 at Dead Man's Corner carries markings (1A-70AD-12) that show it as Tank No 12 (it was of C Company), 70th Tank Battalion, US First Army. This tank was part of a group that included a platoon of Shermans and men of 101st Airborne who were involved in the advance on Saint-Côme-du-Mont from the east—part of a coordinated battleplan which saw two battalions of the 506th PIR attack from the north while 3/501st PIR and 1/401st GIR assaulted from the east. The artillery cover—a 75mm and 105mm barrage—was laid down by 65th Armored FA Battalion, and the 101st's own 377th FA Battalion.

During the confused attack—1/401st were badly held up—the tank was destroyed by a Panzerfaust and the story goes that one of the crew, possibly the commander, died, his body hanging from the tank for some time before he was taken down—long enough for "Dead Man's Corner" to take hold. There's much debate about who the dead man was, but there's no doubt that the ground was held by men of Fallschirmjäger-Regiment 6, whose HQ and aid station was in the building that today houses the Dead Man's Corner Museum. This excellent establishment has been expanded considerably recently and is well worth a visit.

Right and Oppsite: *M5A1 Stuart outside the Dead Man's Corner Museum. Note the deflector over the pintle-mounted .30cal MG atop the turret.*

Location: Saint-Martin-
de-Varreville, Normandy,
France
Commemorating: Gen
Leclerc and 2e DB's arrival
on French soil
Date: August 1, 1944

M8 Greyhound "Koufra" Armored Car, M3 "Temara" Halftrack, and M4A2(75) Sherman "Normandie" Medium Tank

Above Right: *"Temara" is
a heavily restored halftrack,
which was capable of carrying
an infantry squad.*

Below Right: *"Normandie"
served with Third Army and
then took part in the liberation
of Strasbourg. Note the blue
and yellow 2e DB divisional
sign of the Cross of Lorraine
on a backbround of France.*

Opposite: *M8 "Koufra" is
named after the victory in
North Africa where Leclerc
and his men swore not to lay
down their arms before their
colors flew above Strasbourg
cathedral.*

This monument—and the three vehicles around it—celebrates the arrival of the first substantial French forces on French soil on August 1, 1944, as Gen Leclerc's 2nd French Armored Division (2e DB) landed as part of Gen Patton's US Third Army. 2e DB was formed from Free French units that had fought under Leclerc in Africa mixed with other French troops who had flocked to General de Gaulle in the UK. The French had missed the June 6 landings on Omaha Beach and were desperate to return and reclaim their country. On disembarking, 2e DB immediately set out for La Haye du Puits and St James in the southern part of the Département of Manche and went on to play a critical role in the battle to close the Argentan-Falaise Pocket, August 12–21. The division continued through hard fighting from the Normandy breakout to the final assault on Germany and Hitler's Berchtesgaden Eagle's Nest on May 4, 1945, on the way liberating Paris (August 19–25), defeating 112th Panzer Brigade in Lorraine (September), forcing the Saverne Gap through the Vosges mountains (November), and liberating Strasbourg (November 23).

The vehicles around the monument are all American but were issued to 2e DB and bear French insignia. The M8 was a 6x6 armored car with a crew of four. Produced by Ford and used by US, British, Free French, and other Allied troops as a fast reconnaissance vehicle, it was armed with a 37mm main gun and had two Browning machine guns of .30 and .50 calibers. It had a reputation for being fast—top road speed of 55mph (89kph)—but was of limited use across rough country and its thin armor made it vulnerable; nevertheless, it was produced in large numbers.

Chapter 2: Chasing the Enemy Across Europe

Once the Allied bridgehead had been secured, a vast river of men, equipment, and fuel were unloaded to keep the invasion supplied—by the end of August over two million men had been landed. Nevertheless the German coastal forces held up the Allies for some seven weeks before the combination of overwhelming air superiority and resupply began to tell against their tenacious in-depth defense, while their critical armored divisions in the west were consumed in the process, fed piecemeal into the line to shore it up.

Although the Germans were the experts in art of rear-guard fighting withdrawals, Hitler's constant interference was also crucial. His insistence that the bulk of German armor be held back until the exact point of invasion was confirmed; his refusal to let his commanders make tactical withdrawals when required; his most able commander Rommel being wounded, then implicated in the July 20, 1944, bomb plot and forced to commit suicide: these factors contributed to the loss of over 400,000 men—the bulk of German forces committed to the defense of France and all their heavy equipment. July 25 saw the launch of Operation Cobra by US First Army. Having broken out of the difficult Normandy bocage, Patton's Third Army was made operational and sent through the gap to exploit the enemy's rear areas. First, in conjunction with the British Operation Bluecoat, the Germans were cut off in the Falaise Pocket; then Paris was liberated (August 19–25); next the Allies advanced helter-skelter into Belgium and Holland.

In the end, this rapid Allied advance could not be sustained, and the armies paused to regroup, replenish, and for fuel to be brought to the front. This, in turn, gave the Germans time to regroup—with resistance consequently becoming more dogged as the Allies reached the borders of the Reich itself. However, with the Germans now fighting on three fronts the end was inevitable.

M4A1(76)W Sherman "Lucky Forward" Medium Tank

This Sherman is named after and marks the location of General George S. Patton's first Third Army Headquarters in France, used from July 5–August 1, 1944, and called "Lucky Forward." Here, with the aid of Enigma decodes and knowledge of German dispositions, he planned and prepared for the breakout that followed First Army's Operation Cobra. Third Army went operational on August 1 and the rest is history.

The Sherman M4A1(76)W was the first of the 76mm-gunned M4s to be used by US troops themselves. The 76mm gun was produced from February 1944 and so was available in time for the Normandy landings and combat in NW Europe. The British also received it as the Sherman IIA but preferred their own modified Sherman—the Firefly, armed with the QF 17pdr—and so gave the M4A1(76)Ws to the Poles and other Commonwealth Allies fighting alongside them.

To fit the 76mm gun the original M4 chassis required a new turret design that was cast in a single piece—as was the M4A1's hull—and because of muzzle flash problems a muzzle brake was fitted in the M1A1C and later M1A2 versions. "Lucky Forward" has a muzzle brake identifing its gun as an M1A1C. Subsidiary armaments included the usual coaxial and hull-mounted .30cal machine guns, and a .50cal machine gun mounted on top of the turret.

The "W" in this tank's nomenclature signifies another improvement of this model: the wet storage of ammunition on either side of the main drive shaft. With 65 rounds protected by 34.5 gallons of water and another six rounds carried in a rack in the turret floor similarly protected, ammunition fires were considerably reduced if the tank was hit. It was powered by a Continental R975 C4 nine-cylinder radial engine with a top road speed of 30mph and a range of approximately 120 miles.

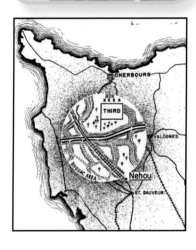

Above: *Location of US Third Army and "Lucky Forward" in July 1944, just outside Néhou, France.*

Right: *Note the Third Army insignia (white A in blue circle bounded in red): of course this is modern.*

Movement date	Location	Miles traveled
Locations of Lucky Forward July 5, 1944, to May 3, 1945		
1944		
5–7 July	Néhou, France	
1 Aug	Legignard, France	25
2–3 Aug	Beauchamps, France	38
8 Aug	Poiley, France	32
12 Aug	St Ouen, France	35
14–15 Aug	La Bazoge, France	67
20 Aug	Brou, France	73
25 Aug	Courcy-aux-Loges, France	68
30 Aug	La Chaume, France	80
4 Sept	Marson, France	99
15 Sept	Braquis, France	68
22 Sept–8 Oct	Etain, France	5
11 Oct	Nancy, France	60
28 Dec	Luxembourg City	90
1945		
27–28 March	Idar-Oberstein, Germany	80
3 April	Frankfurt, Germany	85
11 April	Hersfeld, Germany	85
22 April	Erlangen, Germany	150
2–3 May	Regensburg, Germany	87
TOTAL	19 locations	1,225

Right and Opposite: *The
Churchill Mark VII weighed
in at over 40 tons, most of it
in extra armor that enabled it
to take enormous punishment
—which was just as well given
its poor speed. The Mk VII
was also designed to be
quickly converted to a
Crocodile flamethrower
(A22F) without any major
modifications (see pages 4
and 33).*

A22 Churchill Mk VII Infantry Tank

This Churchill Mk VII was put in place on July 10, 1999, thanks to the efforts of Albert Figg, a gunner in 112 Field Regiment, RA who took part in the Battle for Hill 112. In the British attack—Operation Jupiter over July 10–11— the 43rd (Wessex) Infantry Division was supported by 4th Armoured Brigade. It drew in 10th SS-Panzer Division *Frundsberg* supported by Tigers of sSSPzAbt 102, and forced the recall of 9th SS-Panzer Division *Hohenstaufen* which had been heading westward, in a deliberate attempt to pin down as much German armor as possible and free up the Americans further west. In a grueling battle that lasted all day, the British were forced off the top of the hill and took very heavy casualties, but in the process reduced II SS-Panzer Corps to a condition from which it never recovered. Between June 29, when the 9th and 10th SS-Panzer Divisions regained the hill, and July 23, when they were driven from Maltot, the area around Hill 112 changed hands many times and thousands of Allied and German troops were killed or wounded on its bloody slopes until the Germans retreated after the fall of Caen.

The Churchill Mk VII tank had a crew of five and was armed with an Ordnance QF 75mm gun and two 7.92mm Besa machine guns, one in the hull which had a limited arc of fire due to the protruding front tracks and one in the turret coaxial with the main gun. It was powered by a Bedford horizontally opposed twin-six petrol engine that was very slow, and had a maximum road speed of only 15mph. This version of the Churchill tank was fitted with thicker armor than previous models and is sometimes referred to as the "Heavy Churchill."

M4A4T(75) Sherman "Thunderbolt" Medium Tank

Right: *Lt Col (later General) Creighton Abrams commanded the 37th Tank Battalion of the US 4th Armored Division. An aggressive and successful armor commander, in a similar mold to his US Third Army commander Gen George Patton, his unit was frequently the spearhead of attacks. The US Army's current MBT is named after the one-time US Army Chief-of-Staff.* NARA

Opposite: *M4AT(75) sporting the 4A-37A (37th Tk Bn of 4th Armord Division) markings. The "T" identifies the tank as having been upgraded by the French after WWII and used by the French Army.*

One of the best preserved tanks in Normandy, this M4A4T(75) Sherman in Avranches, bears the set of "Thunderbolt" markings that were on the tank commanded by US Lt Col Creighton Abrams, CO of 37th Tank Battalion of the 4th Armored Division—the unit which first liberated Avranches on July 30, 1944. Part of General Patton's Third Army, 4th Armored set out from Coutances on July 28 with three German divisions retreating ahead of them, mainly two SS divisions: 2nd SS-Panzer *Das Reich*, which had borne the brunt of the Operation Cobra bombing attack, and 17th SS-Panzergrenadier, *Goetz von Berlichingen*, which lost significant numbers of men and vehicles when surrounded by US 2nd Armored in the Roncey Pocket. Under continued air attack, at the village of Gavray 2nd Panzer managed to hold up the advance for a few hours and blew the bridge over the Sienne, but it couldn't hold Third Army.

After the liberation of Avranches Patton's army sped into Brittany in the west and towards the Loire in the east. The Germans tried to cut them off by counterattacking at Mortain: Operation Lüttich. It failed completely and pushed the head of the German forces in Normandy into a noose. As they were outflanked to their south the front in the east collapsed, resulting in many of the German troops in Normandy becoming trapped in the Falaise Pocket.

By this time of the war the 75mm-armed Sherman could compete with a PzKpfw IV but couldn't penetrate the frontal armor of the Panther or Tiger, requiring them to attack from the side or rear and to get close. However, in the relatively tank-free areas behind the front lines, the automotive reliability of the Sherman proved its worth and by the end of August they had advanced farther than their supply lines and reached Metz.

M3A1 Halftrack

M3A1

Location: 54–55 rue Cavee, 61160 Tournai-sur-Dive, France
Commemorating: The end of the Battle of Normandy
Combatants: Canadian Army; German Army
Date: August 21, 1944

Right: *The M3's versatility enabled extensive modification to fit a variety of roles—as an armored personnel carrier, fitted with a howitzer to become a self-propelled gun or given an AA capability as here, with auto cannon or machine guns such as the M45 Quadmount consisting of four M2HB Browning MGs guns mounted in pairs on each side of an open, electrically powered turret.* NARA

Opposite: *M3A1 memorial to the events of August 21, 1944.*

Tournai-sur-Dive sits at the center of the Falaise Pocket and has the distinction of being at the heart of the surrender of the remaining German troops under the direction of the local parish priest Marcel Launay who acted as an intermediary. Hiding with his parishoners in a cellar, Father Launay was ordered out by a German officer. Unsure what his fate would be, the priest was relieved to hear that the Germans wanted to engineer a surrender. After three days of vicious combat more than 2,000 troops and officers laid down their weapons in front of a single Canadian soldier (who arrived in an M3A1) and at 18:30 on August 21, 1944, the battle for Normandy was declared ended. This halftrack in Tournai sports the Canadian Maple Leaf insignia in honor of that moment.

The US M3 halftrack remains one of the most produced American AFVs ever, with over 40,000 made during WWII, to be used by the US and also supplied to all its allies. There were many variations built on the chassis including tank destroyers, mortar carriers and ambulances, but one of the most numerous was the M3A1. Slightly larger than the previous M2A1, it was designed to carry an entire rifle squad of twelve men and their equipment—ten in the back and space for two more with the driver in the cabin—but was multipurpose and could also pull artillery and ammunition. It was armed with a heavy .50cal M2HB Browning attached to an armored pulpit mount above the cabin and two .30cal machine guns with various pintle mount attachment points. It also had a distinctive unditching roller at the front that stopped it from getting stuck in a ditch - the roller preventing the front of the vehicle from digging-in to the opposite face, instead acting as a wide wheel to enable it to climb out more easily. It was powered by a White 160AX engine giving a top speed of 45mph and had a range of 200 miles.

Location: Coudehard-Montormel Memorial, 61160 Mont-Ormel, France
Commemorating: Falaise Gap battles
Combatants: Canadian Army; 1st Polish Armoured Division; 2e DB; US Army,- German Army
Date: August 19–22, 1944

M8 Greyhound Armored Car and M4A1(76) Sherman "Maczuga" Medium Tank

The Coudehard-Montormel Memorial on Mont-Ormel is dedicated to the battle of the Falaise Pocket—the last act in the battle for Normandy. An open-air monument inaugurated in 1965, it sits on the summit of Hill 262, which the Poles called *Maczuga* (the "Mace"), where the pocket was officially closed. A linked museum opened in 1994 on the battle's fiftieth anniversary. Hill 262 sat astride the Germans' only escape route and was defended by 1st Polish Armoured Division who had seized it on August 19. Despite coming under sustained attack, the Poles held it until noon on August 21, thus contributing greatly to the decisive Allied victory. The M4 Sherman on the site sports Polish insignia and the names "Gen Maczek" and "Maczuga." Nearby, is a bust of Gen Stanislaw Maczek, the commander of the 1st Polish Armoured Division.

When the Canadians finally managed to force their way south and link up with the Poles they found a scene of carnage and tragedy. Scattered everywhere were thousands of corpses entangled in burned-out vehicles and disemboweled tanks. In places Polish and German soldiers lay side by side, united in death after their hand-to-hand combat. Of the Poles that had originally arrived, there remained 4 officers out of 60 and 110 men fit to fight out of 1,500—325 were dead. Out of 87 tanks less than 30 were still in a fit state, although only 11 were beyond repair.

The M8 Greyhound on the site carries the colors of the French 2e DB, which was supporting the Poles in the east.

In total 80,000–100,000 German troops were caught in the Falaise Pocket, of whom 10,000–15,000 were killed, 40,000–50,000 were taken prisoner, and 20,000–50,000 escaped.

Right: *M8 Greyhound with the Cross of Lorraine markings. The M8 was a successful armored car armed with a 37mm M6 main gun, a .30cal coaxial MG, and a .50 M2HB on a ring-mount. It could speed along at 55mph on roads.*

Opposite: *The M4A1 is named "Maczuga" on its right flank and "Gen Maczek" on its left.*

Location: La Butte du Sap, 61120 Vimoutiers, France
Commemorating: End of the Battle of the Falaise Pocket and the Battle for Normandy
Combatants: German Army; Allied Armies (US, UK, Canada, Free France, Poland)
Date: August 21, 1944

PzKpfw VI Ausf E Tiger Heavy Tank

On the outskirts of Vimoutiers sits a very rare original survivor from the battle of the Falaise Pocket: a German Tiger. Outside, very much the worse for wear and needing a lot of TLC, it bears the scars—scrap metal dealers had started to cut it up for scrap— and has also been painted by amateur volunteers in a somewhat bizarre approximation of German camouflage. Nevertheless, this tank is the real thing and was part of the *schwere SS-Panzer Abteilung* 102 and originally carried the number 231 on the side of its turret. One of several Tigers on their way to a fuel dump on August 21, 1944, while attempting to escape across the Seine, it ran out of petrol and was abandoned by its crew, who detonated two demolition charges on the engine covers and under the turret. When the Americans took Vimoutiers it was then bulldozed out of the way and left in a ditch to rot. After the war it was sold to a scrap dealer who only removed the gearbox and another later dealer was prevented from breaking the Tiger up further by the residents of Vimoutiers, who decided to purchase the tank themselves in the name of the town.

Although over-engineered and expensive to produce, the Tigers were one of the most powerful tanks of WWII and had a fearsome reputation. The Ausf E weighed 57 tonnes and had armor 100mm at the front, 80mm on the side and 120mm on the gun mantlet. Its main gun was the 88mm KwK 36 L/56 firing the upgraded PzGr 40 APCR ammunition (when it was available), with penetration of up to 200mm at average combat ranges—way beyond any Allied armor. It also had two 7.92mm MG 34 machine guns, one in a ball mount in the hull and the other coaxial with the main gun. It was powered by a Maybach HL230 P45 V-12 engine with a maximum road speed of 28.2mph and had a notional operational range of 68–121 miles, although automotive reliability was suspect.

Right: *Bombing up— ammunition resupply—of a Tiger. The Tiger carried 92 rounds of AP and HE ammunition that used electrically fired primers. Tigers were organized into heavy tank battalions and deployed to critical sectors of any front, either for breakthrough operations or counter-attacks but later in the war they became more defensive, as mobile anti-tank and infantry gun support weapons.* George Forty Collection

Opposite: *There's only one Tiger I freely visible on the roadside, and this is it!*

Location: Resistance Memorial, Avenue de la Resistance, Laxou, Nancy, France
Commemorating: Heroes known and unknown of the Resistance; victims of WWII from overseas; US Army
Date: WWII and September 14, 1944

M4A1(76) Sherman Medium Tank

Right: *Nancy was encircled in a brilliant operation by XII Corps, but the Lorraine campaign soon bogged down in the fall rains.*

Opposite: *On the western outskirts of Nancy, at Laxou on the Toul road, this 4th Armored M4A1 (76mm) stands as a memorial to the liberation of the city. The M4A1(76) Sherman weighed 32.3 tons and was powered by a twin General Motors 6-71 diesel engine giving it a top road speed of almost 30mph with a range of 100 miles and approximately half that for cross-country.*

In front of the Novotel Hotel on the Avenue de La Resistance in the Laxou suburb of Nancy is a site containing a memorial (Resistance Memorial Meurthe-et-Moselle) to the French Resistance. It features a giant Cross of Lorraine, a memorial of two anchors to all victims of WWII from overseas—especially 20 Malagasy soldiers shot at this site by the Germans in 1940 —and finally a US M4A1(76) Sherman tank, restored in 1985.

The tank's serial number of 52457 denotes that it was built in 1944, its larger 76mm gun requiring the larger cast turret. However the M1A1 gun has no muzzle brake and so predates the M1A1C or M1A2 that were later modifications following problems with flash and smoke from the unmuzzled M1A1, making it difficult to track shots. Other improvements included the addition of extra armor plates on the hull and turret gun mantle, a new hull front angle of 47° that both improved frontal protection and simplified production, and the "wet" shell storage system. There were larger access hatches for the driver and co-driver, a loader's hatch, and a vision cupola for the commander replacing the original rotating hatch ring.

The encirclement of Nancy by 4th Armored caused such confusion far behind the German lines that they hastily evacuated the city and US 35th Infantry Division was able to occupy it with little opposition. Gen Manton Eddy likened 4th Armored's CCA's "ride around Nancy" with Jeb Stuart's ride around Richmond in the American Civil War, with the difference that "Clarke's ride" (Col Bruce C. Clarke, later to become famous for his heroic action at St Vith in the Ardennes)had played a key part in causing the fall of the city. At Arracourt and Valhey they overran the HQ of 15th Panzergrenadier Division, capturing or killing its personnel before helping CCB to cross the Marne–Rhin Canal.

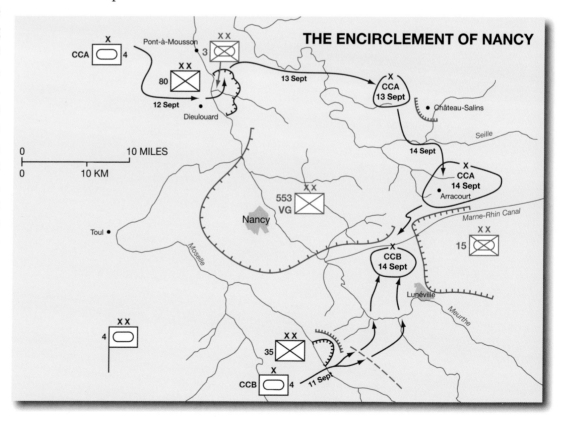

THE ENCIRCLEMENT OF NANCY

Location: 53 Grande Rue, 54370 Arracourt, France
Commemorating: The battle of Arracourt
Combatants: US Army; German Army
Date: September 18–29, 1944

Right: *The M4 Sherman is often underrated, particularly when compared to German armor. However, the battles around Arracourt in mid-September 1944 saw Shermans of 4th Armored blunt the German LVIII Panzer Corps' counter-attack and use their superior speed, maneuverability, and electric turret traverse to great effect. They were helped by the fact that it was most of the German crews' first taste of combat and they were seriously under-trained.*

Opposite: *The M4A4T in Arracourt village is in honor of Maj Gen John S. Wood, commander of the 4th Armd Div, Third Army, winner of the tank battle of Arracourt.*

M4A4T(75) Sherman Medium Tank

At about 07:00 on September 19 Capt William Dwight, liaison officer for the 37th Tank Battalion, was returning to his battalion area near Lezey, which was in the vicinity of Arracourt. It was very foggy, limiting visibility to about 50 yards. As he approached Lezey from the southwest he heard firing ahead. It was a German counterattack!

This US M4A4T Sherman sitting in the center of Arracourt is dedicated to Maj Gen John S Wood, Commander of 4th Armored Division of Gen Patton's US Third Army and victor of the tank battle that raged around the area of this small village September 18–29, 1944. Patton's rapid advance eastwards had halted only when it ran out of fuel and this pause allowed the Germans to surprise the Allies with their ability to launch an unexpected counter-attack.

To continue Capt Dwight's story, being armed with nothing larger than a pistol, he returned to combat command headquarters where a platoon of tank destroyers was made available. Capt Dwight started on the return journey to his battalion, leading his four tank destroyers. Near Bezange he ran head on into another panzer column and lost one tank destroyer in the ensuing firefight. He secured a position on high ground west of Bezange as the fog began to lift and engaged the enemy in a fight that lasted for nearly two hours, during which nine enemy tanks were destroyed while Capt Dwight lost two more destroyers. In spite of being reduced to one tank destroyer and a few dismounted crewmen, Capt Dwight held his position, first against the enemy tank attack and later against an attack by enemy infantry, until the situation cleared enough to permit a limited objective attack by the 37th to extricate his small force from its exposed position. This was an example of the tenacious devotion to duty of all personnel that brought the battle of that day to a successful conclusion.

LVIII PANZER KORPS ATTACK
September 19, 1944

CCA, 4th Armd Div positions am Sept 19
Positions established during the action
Route of approach, German armor
Farthest penetration of German attack
US movements
German front line (approx) pm Sept 19

1000 0 1 2
Yards   Miles

Today sporting Guards Armoured markings, this M4 hull has a Firefly turret and commemorates the hard-fought battle of Hechtel, which took place on September 6–12, 1944. It pitted the Guards Armoured Division against Fallschirmjäger. During the fighting, on September 10, the Guards pushed northeast and captured Joe's Bridge on the Maas–Schelde Canal. This would be the start point for Operation Garden.

Chapter 3: Clearing the Low Countries

Left: *Market Garden depended on British XXX Corps which had to move 20,000 vehicles through 64 miles of enemy territory in three days. The road was easily blocked and ideal for delaying actions. Added to this, the throng of Dutch well-wishers slowed the column down in the larger towns. However, in spite of the problems at Son Bridge (destroyed and a Bailey bridge erected), the heroic efforts of 101st Airborne at Veghel and the 82nd at Grave, meant that by 10:00 on the 19th, the Grenadier Guards were in Nijmegen—behind schedule, but with the sniff of a chance to fulfill the mission. It was not to be and the British Paras at Arnhem bridge entered captivity.* George Forty Collection

Opposite: *The Belgian Brigade Piron (insignia inset) was formed in 1943 and commanded by Lt Col Jean-Baptiste Piron (later Lt Gen, DSO). This monument—with a Staghound turret—is in memory of the soldiers of the Belgian Piron Brigade who fell during the liberation of Leopoldsburg and Heppen on September 11/12 when it fought with BR 8th Armd Div to set up the starting line for Operation Garden.*

Following the liberation of Paris, a mood of euphoria had swept through the Allies with the seductive idea that the war might be over by Christmas. Patton's Third Army had reached the Moselle and other American forces had crossed the border from Luxembourg into Germany itself, while the British and Canadians progressed across Belgium towards Holland. Montgomery now managed to persuade Eisenhower to allow a narrow front punch with his Operation Market Garden—to bypass the Westwall and jump the Rhine.

On September 17 it began with paratroop drops on the bridges over the Maas, the Waal and the lower Rhine at Arnhem. British XXX Corps then pushed forward to link up with them but delays and the speed of the German reaction meant that they never got through. The attack collapsed after 10 days and exaggerated Allied optimism evaporated in the face of this determined German resistance—there would be a hard winter's fighting with many more casualties before they prevailed.

The French Channel ports had been turned into fortresses that had been bypassed by the Allies, who settled on taking Antwerp in order to shorten their now lengthy supply lines. In the Battle of the Scheldt (October 2–November 8) Canadian, British and Polish forces endured a costly struggle against well-prepared German forces fighting an effective delaying action. In the end Antwerp was taken but having been in continuous action since the beginning of June the Allies were suffering from increasing battle exhaustion. As the port reopened and fresh supplies began to stream in from November 28 the Germans vainly fired more V2 rockets at it than any other city in the war.

M4A4 Sherman Firefly Medium Tank

Right: *M5 Stuart of Polish 1st Armoured Division in Tielt, Belgium, against a backdrop still recognizable today.* George Forty Collection

Opposite: *The M4A4 was powered by the extraordinary Chrysler A57 Multibank engine, which combined five inline six-cylinder car engines on a single drive shaft. The resulting 30-cylinder engine was much more complex and the Americans found it unreliable, preferring instead the earlier radial air-cooled engine of the series.*

Inset: *Polish 1st Armoured Division insignia.*

In Generaal Maczekplein square in central Tielt, as part of the WWII Liberation Monument, sits an M4A4 Sherman Firefly, bearing the insignia of the 1st Polish Armoured Division, placed to commemorate their liberation of the town on September 8, 1944. This division, commanded by the very able General Stanislaw Maczek (1892–1994), arrived in Normandy in late July, entering the fight on August 8 during Operation Totalize, and continued the Allied drive across northern France from Falaise to Wilhelmshaven, through Belgium, the Netherlands, and finally Germany. In Belgium they liberated Ardooie, Lotenhulle, Ruiselede, Tielt, Waregem, Wingene, and Zwevezele.

The M4A4 Sherman Firefly was the first Allied tank that was capable of knocking out a German Panther or Tiger at a distance. The original M4A4 was disliked by the US Army mainly because of its large complicated engine, and so it was supplied to Allies and modified by the British with their QF 17pdr gun. The Firefly was produced just in time for the D-Day landings but not in sufficient numbers to replace the other Shermans used by the British and Commonwealth forces. A single Firefly was used to provide heavier support in a troop of four tanks, with the three other Shermans armed with the less powerful 75mm gun. Although this extra firepower put the Firefly on more level terms with German heavy tanks, its own armor was still thin and it remained highly vulnerable.

M4A4 Sherman Firefly Medium Tank

Right: *Bombing up a Firefly. It carried 77 rounds but many were difficult to get to in combat.* George Forty Collection

Opposite: *In 1984 Lt Gen Roger Dewandre, who had fought in Normandy and the Low Countries and been Deputy Chief of the Belgian General Staff in the 1970s, promised Leopoldsburg a Sherman tank as a monument to remember its role in Operation Market Garden. The tank had been used as a target on the Brasschaat firing range where another vehicle supplied missing parts. The inauguration was on October 5, 1984.*

This British M4A4 Sherman Firefly with the Guards Armoured Division insignia painted on the bottom right of the glacis was originally located in the center of nearby Hechtel, but was moved here in 2009 and commemorates the British forces who took part in Operation Market Garden. It was not originally a Firefly and the turret was added later—it may even have been a Sherman Dozer for it still has some of the dozer fittings.

The Firefly was armed with the British QF 17pdr—a 76.2mm gun with a length of 55 calibres. It had a 2,900ft/sec muzzle velocity firing HE and HEAT rounds and 3,950ft/sec when firing APDS or SPC and APCBC munitions. This enabled it to defeat armor 120–208mm (4.72–8.18in) thick at a range of 3,000ft and up to 4,500ft with the APDS. A Vickers engineer, W.G.K. Kilbourn, managed to cram the heavy gun into a turret it was never designed for and by doing so enabled the quick conversion of the most prolifically produced American tank, the Sherman. The turret interior was completely modified, with the rear being emptied to allow the gun its recoil of one metre, a new recoil system fitted and a counterweight added to the rear to balance the long barrel. The mantlet was also thickened, the loader's position changed and a new hatch cut over the gunner's position and there were a few changes made to the chassis with the hull gunner position eliminated to make room for the giant 17pdr shells. More than 2,100 Fireflies were produced and used by the 4th, 8th, 27th, and 33rd Armoured Brigades, the Guards Armoured Division and the 1st, 6th, 7th, and 11th Armoured Divisions in Normandy, northwestern Europe and Italy. The Canadians, Czechoslovaks, New Zealanders, Poles, and South Africans all used them, too.

Location: Oude Staatsbaan,
9900 Eeklo, Belgium
Commemorating: All
Canadian Liberators
Combatants: Canadian
Army; German Army
Date: September 15, 1944

M4A4(75) Sherman "Clanky" Medium Tank

Commissioned in 1990 by the municipality of Eeklo and dedicated in 1992 to all Canadian units who fought so hard for the liberation of the town and all Belgium, this M4A4 Sherman (complete with both its hull and coaxial machine guns) sits next to Balgerhoeke lock. Following its installation and unsure of its exact origin, it was a joint Canadian and Belgian decision to give the tank very specific insignia, in order to tie it to a Canadian regiment and validate the memorial still further.

On September 15, 1944, the first tanks to enter Eeklo were a section of the Recce Troop and C Squadron of the South Alberta Regiment (commanded by Colonel Gordon Wotherspoon), part of the 4th Canadian Armoured Division, so the tank was given their respective markings. The green and blue square indicates arm of service (reconnaissance) and the 45 indicates the South Alberta Regiment; the formation sign of the 4th Canadian Armoured Division is the gold maple leaf on a green background). Within the white circle on the turret is the number 19 and this is a reference to an officer in the South Alberta Regiment at the time: Major David Currie, VC, the only Canadian soldier to whom a Victoria Cross was awarded during the Normandy campaign, and the only Victoria Cross ever awarded to a member of the Royal Canadian Armoured Corps. Maj Currie's tank was known as "Clanky," the name on the side of this M4A4. On Monday, July 29, 2013, a large Canadian delegation was officially welcomed at the City Hall of Eeklo, Belgium for the rededication ceremony of the now firmly identified Sherman.

Right: *Note the 45 (arm of service sign) at left and golden maple leaf on a green background at right.*

Opposite: *The markings identify "Clanky"—the vehicle of Major David Currie, the RCAC's only VC winner.*

Achilles Mk IIC Self-Propelled Gun

ACHILLES Mk IIC

Location: Canada and Poland WW II Museum, Heulendonk 21, Maldegem, Belgium
Commemorating: The liberation of Belgium by the Canadians and Poles.
Combatants: Canadian Army; 1st Polish Armoured Division; German Army
Date: September–December 1944

Just outside the beautiful grounds of the Canadian and Polish World War II Museum near Heulendonk sits an Achilles IIC carrying no insignia. The liberation of Belgium and the bitter battles around the Scheldt estuary fell primarily to the First Canadian Army, which also had some British, Polish, and other troops under its command. For the Canadians it was some of their most difficult fighting of the war, and casualties were heavy.

The Achilles began life as the US M10 Wolverine made at the Fisher Tank Arsenal in Grand Blanc, Michigan. It was based on the chassis and running gear of the M4 series but with thinner, more sloped armor that made it quicker than the Sherman, with a top speed of 32mph. Those intended for British and Commonwealth use were converted by the Royal Arsenal at Woolwich into the Achilles using their own Ordnance QF 17pdr artillery gun modified to fit into an enclosed turret that required a counterweight just behind the muzzle-brake of its long barrel. This was a distinctive feature that crews of the Achilles (and the similarly main-gunned Firefly) tried to hide with *trompe l'oeil* camouflage so as not to attract undue attention from the Germans who, knowing their capabilities and weaknesses, sought to dispose of them swiftly whenever they could.

Formed into AT batteries in armored divisions' or corps' AT regiments, the Canadians used the Achilles in the same way as the British: as a tank destroyer that could keep up with an attack and hold taken ground against counter-attacks. Hull down and hiding its thin armor, with time to hand crank its manually operated turret, the Achilles was a dangerous weapon that had the measure of all but the thickest German armor. All told some 1,100 M10s were converted into the Achilles and it was the second most produced AFV armed with the QF 17pdr gun after the Sherman Firefly.

Opposite: *The Achilles Mk IC used an M10/M4A2 chassis; the IIC used an M10A1/M4A3.*

Above Left: *A Canadian TD—a 17pdr Achilles or 105mm M10—with its turret in traveling postion, facing the rear (note counterweight).*

Below Left: *Infantrymen of Le Régiment de la Chaudière riding on an M10A1 3rd AT Regiment, Royal Canadian Artillery during the attack on Elbeuf, France, August 26, 1944.* Both: Dept. of National Defence/Library and Archives Canada/Below: Lt Donald Grant, PA-190211

M4A1(75) Sherman Medium Tank

This Canadian M4A1 Sherman was placed in the center of Woensdrecht in 1978 to commemorate the heavy fighting that took place here on October 13–18, 1944. Its markings and number (52) indicate a tank of the 10th Canadian Armoured Regiment (Fort Garry Horse), one of very few armored units that were supporting the Canadian infantry in what became a horrible carnage more reminiscent of the First World War, as they repeatedly attacked the well-equipped and seasoned German Fifteenth Army units that had had the time to dig in on both sides of the Scheldt estuary. In their rush to get over the Rhine and deep into Germany, Montgomery and Eisenhower had hoped to bypass the Scheldt and the Canadians paid a heavy price for it: especially the Black Watch (Royal Highland Regiment) of Canada but also the Royal Hamilton Light Infantry—to whose memory the site and the panels below are dedicated. Both received battle honors for this savage engagement.

Woensdrecht was on the causeway that led to South Beveland, the objective of the 2nd Canadian Infantry Division. The plan was to establish a firm base here before pushing west to occupy South Beveland before taking Walcheren.

Friday, October 13, 1944, will always be "Black Friday" to the Black Watch of Canada, as it attacked the dug-in Germans through the polders west of Woensdrecht. When the dust settled, the regiment had suffered 145 casualties, including 56 dead, among them all four company commaders. On October 16, the Royal Hamilton Light Infantry, with tank support, took the village but—reinforced by Paratroopers under Oberst von der Heydte—the Germans counterattacked. It would take five days of intense fighting before the Germans were forced to retreat.

The Scheldt was cleared by November 8, but the Canadians lost of 6,000 casualties.

M4A1(75) SHERMAN

Location: Onderstal 39, 4631 NN Hoogerheide, Netherlands
Commemorating: Battle of Woensdrecht
Combatants: Canadian Army; German Army
Date: October 13–18, 1944

Opposite: *Built by the Lima Locomotive Works, #30419403 was used by the Dutch Army after the war.*

Below, Left and Right:
Two panels nearby the tank. The official Canadian WWII history discusses the lack of infantry at the time: "The Canadian Black Watch on 19 October calculated that in the battalion's rifle companies, then 379 all ranks in strength, there were 159 men with three months or more of infantry training; 46 with two months or more; 131 with one month, 29 with less than one month and 14 with none." Their opponents complained, too, about "246 untrained recruits of the ages of 17 and 18 had arrived: 'combat value zero'."

M4A1(75) Sherman "Able Abe" Medium Tank

M4A1 SHERMAN "ABLE ABE"

Location: Oorlogsmuseum, Museumpark 1, 5825 AM Overloon, Netherlands
Commemorating: US 7th Armored Division
Combatants: US Army; German Army
Date: October 1944

"Able Abe" sits in front of the War Museum at Liberty Park in the East Brabant town of Overloon and marks the spot of an intense and bloody battle that raged here for three weeks in the autumn of 1944, as the Allies pushed to capture the German bridgehead at Venlo and push them back across the Maas. The museum opened on May 25, 1946, making it one of the oldest in Europe dedicated to WWII. On September 27, 2008, a monument was inaugurated to the US 7th Armored Division and on October 8, 2011, a Sherman tank recovered from artillery range at Oldenbroek was added to the memorial. 7th Armored had landed at Utah and fought its way through France as part of US Third Army.

On September 25, 1944, it transferred to the US Ninth Army and was assigned to protect the right flank of Operation Market Garden. On September 30 the 7th attacked the Germans at Overloon in what was to become another vicious battle of attrition. For nine days, the American tanks tried to breach the German defenses, but were held and repelled by German mines, artillery and Panther tanks. The assault eventually failed and on October 8 the 7th was switched to a diversionary attack south of Overloon with the British Second Army, while the British 3rd Infantry and 11th Armoured Divisions continued the attack on the town. Their combat began on October 11 and Overloon was eventually taken on October 18, after incurring significant casualties and the town being completely destroyed in the process. It was one of the bloodiest battles that took place in the Netherlands during the WWII as a determined German resistance blunted the Allied thrust. After the ferocity of Overloon and Venray battles the Allies were forced to pause and recoup before pressing on.

Opposite: *"Able Abe."*

Above Left: *Operation Aintree included the largest tank battle in Dutch history, outside Overloon. Vehicles left on the battlefield formed the basis for the War Museum at Liberty Park. The sign at the entrance reads: "Take pause visitor, and consider that the ground you stand on was once one of the most fiercely contested sectors of the Overloon battlefield. Bitter hand-to-hand combat took place here. Many young lives, having escaped from the battlefields of Nettuno and Normandy, met their ends under these trees."*

Below Left: *US 7th Armored memorial next to "Able Abe."*

PzKpfw V Ausf D Panther Medium Tank

Right: *Bombarding Geysteren Castle are a Churchill and "Cuckoo," a 107 Panzer-Brigade Panther captured during the battle of Overloon. It was used by the Coldstream Guards to bombard the castle, and later during Operation Blackcock where its maneuverability in icy conditions as well as the accuracy of its main armament were noticeable.* NARA

Opposite: *Recently repainted, the Panther at Breda was presented to the city by Polish 1st Armoured Division.*

This German PzKpfw V Ausf D Panther sits in the Dutch city of Breda at the junction of Wilhelminapark and Paule Windhausenweg in Southern Holland. It was donated by troops of the Polish 1st Armoured Division to serve as a memorial to their liberation of Breda in 1944—achieved without any civilian casualties. Up until 2004 the tank was in its original condition, but then during a restoration to become part of the current monument the entire remaining interior and engine were removed to be used to get another Panther back in running order. The exterior was then preserved by a special coating and resprayed in its original camouflage paint before being placed on a pedestal to protect the bottom from moisture.

The PzKpfw V Ausf D was the first production version of the Panther and was rushed into combat only a year after being designed. As a result early versions were mechanically unreliable and often recalled for modifications and the Panther's first offensive appearance at Kursk on the Eastern front was a disappointment. However, once these had been sorted out it went on to earn a fearsome reputation as a defensive weapon, with its long-barreled 7.5cm KwK42 L/70 main gun having a kill range of 2,000 yards. Its distinctive sloping armor was as a direct result of the T-34 and increased its overall effectiveness. It was powered by a Maybach HL230P30 engine giving it a top speed of 30mph and a range of 135 miles. Ausf Ds can be identified by two main features: a straight-sided drum-shaped commander's cupola with viewports for periscopes low down on the side, and the lack of a hull machine gun mount, with the machine gun being fired instead through a narrow slit in the hull front.

4 COMMANDO BRIGADE
BRITISH LIBERATION ARMY
LANDDE HIER OP
1 NOV. 1944
OM HET EILAND TE BEVRIJDEN

4 COMMANDO BRIGADE
BRITISH LIBERATION ARMY
LANDED HERE ON
1 NOV. 1944
TO LIBERATE THE ISLAND

OP 3 EN 29 OCT. 1944 WERD DEZE DIJK
DOOR GEALLIEERDE BOMMEN DOORBROKEN
TERWILLE VAN DE BEVRIJDING VAN WALCHEREN
WESTKAPELLE WERD VERWOEST
WALCHEREN DOOR DE ZEE OVERSPOELD
1 NOV. LANDING DER GEALLIEERDEN
8 NOV. WALCHEREN BEVRIJD
3 OCT. 1945 DIJKGAT GEDICHT
WALCHEREN KAN HERRIJZEN

TO THE GREATER GLORY OF
GOD THIS STONE IS ERECTED
BY THE ROYAL MARINES IN
COMMEMORATION OF THE
LANDING of No. 4 COMMANDO
BRIGADE AT WESTKAPELLE ON
1st NOVEMBER 1944

M4A4(75) Sherman V Crab "Bramble 5" Flail Tank

M4A4 SHERMAN V CRAB

Location: Zeedijk, Westkapelle, Walcheren, the Netherlands
Commemorating: British landings at Westkapelle
Combatants: British Army; German Army
Date: November 1, 1944

Below: *Sherman Crab knocked out on D-Day. It affords a good view of the flail rollers. There were at least 40 chains attached.* George Forty Collection

This British M4A4 Sherman Crab marks the spot where the troops landed at Westkapelle on Walcheren on November 1, 1944. On the back of the tank a dedicatory text gives its details. "Bramble 5" is a Sherman V (M4A4) equipped with a 75mm gun and flail equipment to clear mines. It was crewed by men of 1st Lothians & Border Horse. It was employed in the Allied landing of RM Commandos and disembarked from LCT 737 at high tide in the middle of the Zuidstraat on the night of November 1–2, 1944. It bogged down after landing and was unable to continue the attack.

The Sherman Crab or Flail was one of Gen Percy Hobart's "Funnies"—tanks modified to suit a variety of aggressive purposes beyond a normal tank's main gun potential, though they usually kept these as well. The Crab, had a rotating drum held by support arms at a distance in front of the tank. As the drum rotated the chains flailed and set off any mines in its path, clearing a space 9ft wide. Flails were regularly used in combination to clear a broad lane across a minefield, often in the face of enemy fire.

The Sherman Crab became the most widely used mine flail tank of the war as its drive train had no problems powering the flail. Two types were produced, based on different Sherman production models, and they were used extensively during the Allied advances of 1944–1945 in Western Europe. The flail extension increased the tank's overall length from 19.7ft to 26.25ft and later versions had cutting disks on the roller which allowed the tank to slice through barbed wire.

The attack was strongly contested and the invading fleet suffered badly before its ultimate success. The heavily defended capital, Vlissingen, fell three days later.

Opposite: *Sherman Crab on the Westkapelle dyke. The text says:*

Left panel: 4 Commando Brigade, British Liberation Army, landed here on 1 Nov. 1944 to liberate the island.

Center panel: On 3rd and 29th October 1944 this dike was bombed by the Allies for the liberation of Walcheren. The city of Westkapelle was destroyed. The city of Walcheren was washed away by the sea. 1 Nov. 1944 The landing of the Allies; 8 Nov. 1944 Walcheren was liberated; 3 Oct. 1945 hole in dyke was repaired. WALCHEREN CAN ARISE

Right panel: To the greater glory of God this stone is erected by the Royal Marines in commemoration of the landing of No 4 Commando Brigade at Westkapelle on 1st November 1944.

M4A1(75) Grizzly "Robin Hood" Medium Tank

Right: *Note the markings—*
• *red fox on yellow = 8th Armoured Brigade;*
• *996 = Nottinghamshire Sherwood Rangers Yeomanry;*
• *white diamond = Regimental HQ*
• *52 = the second regiment of the brigade (50 = Brigade HQ; 51 = senior regiment; etc).*

Opposite: *"Robin Hood" on its plinth outside the National Liberation Museum.*

This Canadian M4A1 Sherman Grizzly bears the name "Robin Hood" and carries the insignia of the Nottinghamshire Sherwood Rangers Yeomanry. In front of it is a plaque commemorating the 268 soldiers of the Sherwood Rangers who were killed in World War II as well as all soldiers and civilians who perished in the war. Another nearby memorial remembers Operation Market Garden and the Allied spring offensive of 1945 when over 400,000 British and Canadian soldiers, commanded by Canadian General Harry Crerar, cleared the Rhineland up to Wesel, allowing Allied armies to cross the Rhine and end the war.

The Grizzly was a Canadian-built Sherman made at the Montreal Locomotive Works beginning in August 1943. Some 1,200 Grizzlies were originally intended, but by 1944 American Sherman production had kicked into such an overdrive that made it a much easier option for the Canadians to accept the American-produced ones instead.

The Grizzly did differ from its M4A1 origins by having CPD-type (Canadian dry pin) tracks and thicker armor protection. It retained the Continental R-975-C1 nine-cylinder radial engine that produced an output of 353hp at 2,400rpm. Performance was very similar, with a top speed of 24mph and a maximum range of 120 miles. It carried a 75mm high-velocity M3 L/40 main gun mounted in a fully traversable turret and secondary armament of an AAMG (a Browning .50cal M2HB) and two .30cal machine guns—one coaxial with the main gun in the turret and the other bow-mounted in the front right hull.

The Grizzly had a crew of five: commander, loader, gunner, bow-gunner/co-driver and driver. In the end some 200 Grizzlies were produced before the program was halted in January 1944. Remaining hulls and chassis were then used without turrets in the development of some of the first armored personnel carriers used first during Operation Totalize.

Ram Kangaroo APC

This Canadian Ram Kangaroo APC, dedicated to 1st Canadian Armoured Carrier Regiment (1CACR), is a rare beast: this is the only one to be found on public highways in Europe. 1CACR was formed in Tilburg, Holland in August 1944 and disbanded in Enschede on June 20, 1945, with battle honors for North-West Europe 1944–45 including the Lower Maas, the Ruhr, the Rheinland, the Reichswald, Moyland Wood, and Goch-Calpar Road. The development of the APC was a Canadian innovation which, having been made initially from old M3 Stuarts and M7 Priests, next made use of the hull and chassis of a defunct Canadian cruiser tank called the Ram. They were converted at No 1 Canadian Base Workshop of the Royal Canadian Electrical and Mechanical Engineers, located at Bordon Camp, Hampshire, England. This consisted of the removing the turret completely, along with the turret ring and the internal ammunition bins as well any unnecessary hull fittings in order to make enough space to accommodate 10 fully equipped infantrymen. The ball-mounted hull .30cal Browning machine gun was kept or else mounted in the cupola-equipped auxiliary turret, depending on what was already there. Rams had a crew of two and were equipped with the No 19 Wireless Set, and retained their intercom system so that the crew could communicate with each other and the infantry behind them. They were 19ft long, 9ft wide, and 6.5ft high and weighed 24 tons—5 tons lighter than the turreted original. This lower silhouette and lighter weight reduced track pressure and made the vehicle more maneuverable over soft ground. It was powered by a 450hp Continental R975/C1 radial air-cooled nine-cylinder engine, with gave a maximum speed of 25mph and a range of 144 miles.

RAM KANGAROO

Location: Langenboomseweg 4, Mill-en-St-Hubert, North Brabant, the Netherlands
Commemorating: 1st Canadian Armoured Carrier Regiment
Date: August 1944– June 1945

Opposite: *The 1CACR memorial.*

Left: *Ram Kangaroo APCs during the assault by 15th (Scottish) Infantry Division on Blerick, December 3. Through lanes in minefields cleared by flails (22nd Dragoons), over an anti-tank ditch bridged by Churchill AVLBs (81st Assault Engineers), in spite of the mud, the APCs delivered their occupants (Royal Scots Fusiliers) on the outskirts of Blerick, which fell quickly thanks to an inspired attack plan by General Cummings.* NARA

Chapter 4: Battle of the Bulge

There are currently nine turrets on the main roads out of Bastogne, this one—on the way to the Mardasson Memorial—is a T23 with 10th Armored markings and a shell penetration on its left side.

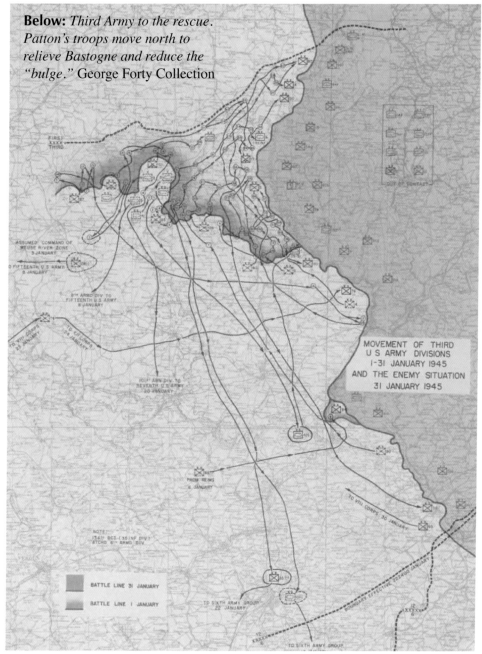

Below: *Third Army to the rescue. Patton's troops move north to relieve Bastogne and reduce the "bulge."* George Forty Collection

MOVEMENT OF THIRD
U S ARMY DIVISIONS
1-31 JANUARY 1945
AND THE ENEMY SITUATION
31 JANUARY 1945

BATTLE LINE 31 JANUARY

BATTLE LINE 1 JANUARY

Above: *Tracks in the snow. 6th Armored battles through Bizory, north of Bastogne.* NARA

On December 16, 1944, Hitler launched his last desperate operation on the Western front—codenamed Wacht am Rhein—in an attempt to split the Allied armies and retake Antwerp. To him it seemed that a critical fault line existed between the British and American military commands, and that a determined assault might shatter this alliance. There was indeed a fundamental difference between the Supreme Commander Eisenhower's broad front strategy and Montgomery's narrow front approach that had led to Operation Market Garden, and Monty was certainly a difficult man to get along with and was disliked by many US commanders. The German attack totally surprised the Allies, as two panzer armies suddenly struck through the snow-covered pine forests of the Ardennes and taking advantage of the appalling winter weather that grounded Allied air support, 400,000 men and over 1400 tanks suddenly punched through the weakest point of the Allied line. The attack was initially extremely successful, killing or capturing over 100,000 US troops and creating a 50 mile salient that gave the conflict its name coined by the press - the Battle of the Bulge. In the end, primarily through tenacious American defense, the German advance was held at St Vith, Elsenborn Ridge, Houffalize, and Bastogne. This blocked vital access to key roads that the German attack depended on for success, instead bunching their forces together and slowing them down considerably, which in turn gave the Allies time to reinforce the thinly held parts of their own line. As the atrocious weather lifted Allied air assets were then brought to bear on both the leading German formations and their rear supply lines with devastating results. German casualties totalled 125,000 men, while the Americans lost 20,000 killed and 60,000 wounded. Although Hitler had again delayed the Allied advance he had used up all his reserves and the Luftwaffe had been almost completely destroyed. German forces now fell back to the Siegfried Line.

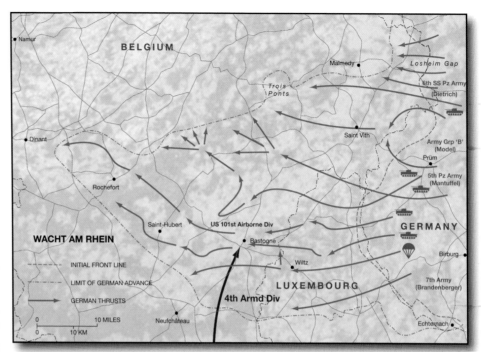

Left and Below: *The Battle of the Bulge began in poor weather negating the Allied air superiority. As the front that was over England on the 16th approached Belgium, rain began. Heavy mists hung over the forest. However, the weather broke for five days beginning on December 23 and once more the bombers and fighter-bombers could fly—to devastating effect as this bombed Panther attests.* NARA

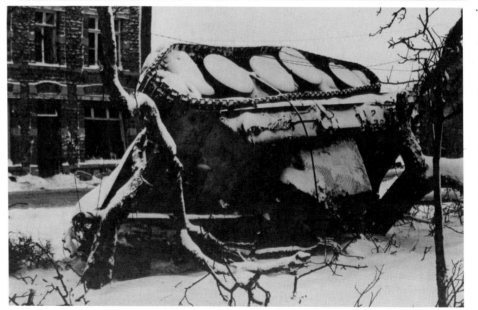

Outside are a number of guns and an M4A3(76) of B/2nd Tank Battalion, 9th Armored, one of five tanks supporting 28th Infantry Division. This one fired at Germans on the Marnach road, retreating behind cover after he had done so. Hit twice but still functioning, the tank was abandoned after it reversed into the house it was using as cover. Subsequently another German round pierced the turret.

M4A3(76) Sherman Medium Tank

M4A3(76) SHERMAN

Location: Château de Clervaux, Clervaux, Luxembourg
Commemorating: Battle of Clervaux
Combatants: US Army; German Army
Date: December 16–18, 1944

The plaque close by this US Sherman M4A3(76) states that it is the only known surviving combat vehicle of the US 9th Armored Division from the battle that took place here on December 17, 1944, when it was put out of action while defending Clervaux at the gate to the castle. Clervaux was the first tank battle of the Germans last attack in the West, now known as the Battle of the Bulge. In Clervaux the Americans (2nd and 707th Tank Battalions; 630th Tank Destroyer Battalion) were initially taken completely by surprise, quickly overwhelmed by 2nd Panzer Division, and forced to surrender after their ammunition ran out in a last ditch stand by 100 men and tanks at the castle. Although the Germans won this engagement the stubborn defense put up by some of the previously untested new troops across this suddenly active front was enough to critically slow their timetable until the weather cleared

and Allied air power ensured the ultimate failure of the operation. This M4A3(76) was from Company B, 2nd Tank Battalion and its serial number of 43911 denotes that it was built in May 1944. The M4A3(76) addressed the problem of small drivers' hatches with its single-piece cast hull and similarly single-mold larger turret with back ventilator for the new 76mm main gun. It used the VVSS (Vertical Volute Spring Suspension) which battle experience showed had a relatively short life, leading to the development of HVSS (Horizontal Volute Spring Suspension). It also had the fireproofing wet stowage system for the main-gun ammunition under the hull floor with a similar six-round ready rack mounted on the turret basket floor. With the addition of HVSS this model of Sherman would go on to become that preferred by the US Army, who continued to use it up until the end of the Korean War.

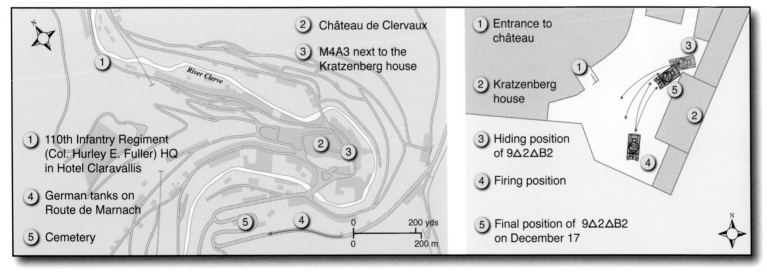

2 Château de Clervaux

3 M4A3 next to the Kratzenberg house

1 110th Infantry Regiment (Col. Hurley E. Fuller) HQ in Hotel Claravallis

4 German tanks on Route de Marnach

5 Cemetery

River Clerve

200 yds
200 m

1 Entrance to château

2 Kratzenberg house

3 Hiding position of 9△2△B2

4 Firing position

5 Final position of 9△2△B2 on December 17

Left: *Clervaux (Clerf in German) stood directly on the XLVII Panzer Corps route towards Bastogne on the lower of Fifth Panzer Army's* Rollbahnen. *During the battle with 2nd Panzer Division, a handful of 28th Infantry Division soldiers, led by Capt John Aitken, were besieged on December 17—the so-called "Luxembourg Alamo." (Drawings based on those from Diorama-Clervaux.)*

PzKpfw VI Ausf B Königstiger Heavy Tank

Location: Outside December 1944 Historical Museum, Rue de l'Eglise 7, La Gleize, Belgium
Commemorating: Battle of the Bulge
Combatants: US Army; 1st SS-Panzer Division *Leibstandarte*
Date: December 1944

Right: *In the end, lacking fuel and ammunition, and under continuous artillery bombardment, Peiper left La Gleize and his heavy weapons, including six Tiger IIs—this one, #334, on the Borgoûmont road.* NARA

Opposite: *Today, La Gleize is a site of pilgrimage for armor fans as it boasts the only Tiger II visible to the public from the roadside, one of only seven survivors of the 489 built. #213 was disabled while sited near Wérimont Farm, to the south of the village.*

This rare surviving German King Tiger was disabled on December 19, 1944 during the Battle of the Bulge in the Belgian Ardennes, when it backed into and brought down a building on itself. It now sits in the village square of La Gleize, opposite the church and outside the December 1944 Historical Museum, established to tell the Battle of the Bulge's local story. Kampfgruppe Peiper's advance was halted here and it abandoned 135 armored vehicles in La Gleize—including SS-Obersturmführer Wilhelm Dollinger's PzKpfw VI Ausf B Königstiger, turret number 213, of *schwere SS-Panzer-Abteilung* 501. Their supply route had been cut, they had run out of vital fuel and ammunition and the Americans were concentrating overwhelming firepower onto their positions.

Even now the King Tiger is a colossal and impressive tank. Over 24ft long, 12ft wide, and 10ft high, sleek with sloped armor and weighing over 70 tons. Its long-barreled high-velocity KwK43 88mm cannon used Pzgr 39/43 armor-piercing ammunition which could penetrate five inches of armor at a range of over a mile. It was also more agile than it looked, with a road speed of about 25mph and a cross-country speed of about 10mph. However, it did suffer from reliability issues, especially at the hands of the poorly trained and inexperienced tank drivers of the late WWII German army. Although a formidable AFV, fewer than 500 King Tigers were produced at the Henschel assembly plant between January 1944 and March 1945—too small a number and too late to have any effect on the outcome of battles on either the Eastern or Western fronts. A lot of German productivity was sacrificed in the search for bigger and better weapons systems, that were inevitably swamped in the quantity produced by both the USSR and the US as the war became increasingly one of resources and production.

Right: *Memorial in Bastogne's Place McAuliffe to the general.*

Opposite: *"Barracuda" served in Company B, 41st Tank Battalion, 11th Armoured Division. It was knocked out near Renaumont, west of Bastogne, on December 30.*

Both: Peter Anderson

M4A3(75)W Sherman "Barracuda" Medium Tank

Sitting in a corner of the Place du General McAuliffe in the center of Bastogne in Belgium is the M4A3(75)W Sherman "Barracuda," from B Company of the US 11th Armored Division's 41st Tank Battalion. It was put out of action near Renaumont, a few kilometers west of Bastogne, on December 30, 1944. Two weeks before more than 200,000 German troops and over 1,400 tanks had begun the Reich's last gamble in the West, surprising and breaking through the American front in the Ardennes Forest, cutting off and surrounding pockets of US troops. Many prisoners were taken—and some mistreated or murdered—however others, isolated and in severe winter conditions, stubbornly dug in. At the critical road junctions of St Vith and Bastogne, American tanks and paratroopers fought off repeated attacks and when the acting commander of the 101st Airborne Division in Bastogne, Brig Gen Anthony McAuliffe, was ordered by his German adversary to surrender, he responded (and became famous for it) with a single-word reply: "Nuts!" In the end the Americans held, Patton's Third Army relieved Bastogne, and the US 2nd Armored Division stopped the German attack short of the River Meuse. The subsequent history of the "Barracuda" crew is known. In attempting to find its unit it got lost, stuck in a frozen pond, and was attacked and disabled by grenades in the turret and a 75mm shell from the side. The commander later died of his wounds. The gunner and loader were also wounded then transferred to a Stalag prisoner-of-war camp. When the Germans discovered that the driver and co-driver were Jewish they were used as slave workers for heavy labor, although both survived. After the war the owner of the pond, fearing contamination, refused permission to cut up the tank but instead gave it to the Belgian Army in 1947. It was then restored, given a new turret complete with a top-mounted .50cal Browning machine gun and returned to the town of Bastogne.

M4A3(76)W Sherman Medium Tank

M4A3 (76)W SHERMAN

Location: Rue de l'Eglise, Beffe, Belgium
Commemorating: Task Force Hogan
Combatants: US Army; German Army
Date: December 1944

The almost vestigial remains of this US M4A3 (76)W Sherman bears two plaques side by side. One is from the municipality of Rendeux that thanks the brave American liberators of January 1945 and calls for "No More War." The other is dedicated to Task Force (TF) Hogan of 3rd Armored Division, which consisted of: HQ 3rd Bn, 33rd Armd Regt; A Co 33rd Armd Regt; A Co 83rd Rcn Bn; 1st Plat C Co 83rd Rcn Bn; A Battery, 54 FA Bn; Section of 486th AAA Bn. On December 22, 1944, TF Hogan "repulsed repeated attacks by overwhelming enemy forces. Low on supplies, the TF fought through enemy lines from here to Marcouray on 25 December. Out of fuel, ammunition and surrounded by three German Divisions TF Hogan destroyed its equipment, infiltrated enemy lines and rejoined 3rd Armored Division."

In fact this Sherman belonged to the 1st or 2nd Platoon of C Company of the 771st Tank Battalion which was attached to 334th Infantry Regiment of the 84th Division. Battling in atrocious winter conditions, the division repulsed German attacks, recaptured Verdenne on December 24–28 and took Beffe and Devantave (Rendeux) on January 4–6, 1945. During a move from Magoster to Marcouray on January 8, 1945 this Sherman slipped on the icy road and slid into a ditch. When the tank was being recovered it then hit a daisy chain of mines which set it on fire, with one crew member killed and three others injured. The tank was then left rotting away in the ditch between Magoster and Beffe until 1984 when it was recovered and placed on a plinth as a monument in Beffe itself. It has no wheels or tracks—the bogies were destroyed in the fire that ensued from the mine strike—and the engine-deck doors are not the original ones but salvaged later from a range wreck.

Right and Far Right: *Plaques on Beffe's M4A3.*

Opposite: *The Beffe M4A3.*

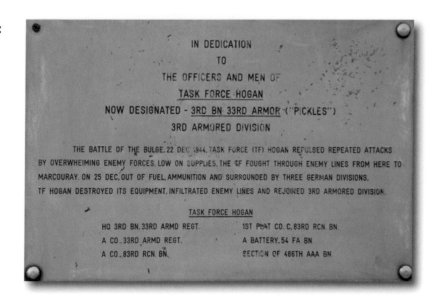

M4A1(76)W Sherman Medium Tank

M4A1(76)W SHERMAN

Location: Rue Vieille Chavée, Vielsalm
Commemorating: 7th Armored Division and all who fought at St Vith
Combatants: US Army; German Army
Date: December 17–23, 1944

Above Right: *7th Armored Division defenses alongside the railroad bridge at Vielsalm.* NARA

Below Right: *The M4A1(76) in Vielsalm has a plaque that remembers* "LE CHAR INVINCIBLE LE COURAGE INVINCIBLE" *[The Invincible Tank The Invincible Courage].*

Right: *This 7th Armored Division memorial can be found in Place General Bruce C. Clarke.*

Opposite: *The M4A1(76) in Vielsalm.*

This M4A1(76) Sherman was another tank left behind by the Americans in December 1944 following the fighting around St Vith. The plaque dedicated in June 1984 "to all who fought so valiantly at St Vith" is mounted on the front hull and commemorates "the US 7th Armored Division and attached units. Headquartered in Vielsalm during the critical period of the German Ardennes offensive in 1944 they held the important center of St Vith, preventing any advance and exploitation on this main line thus frustrating the German offensive by its sacrifice, permitting the launching of the Allied counter-offensive." US General Bruce Clarke, Combat Command A (CCA) of the US 4th Armored Division (who led the initial relief of St Vith during the battle, which critically slowed the German attack) first offered a Sherman to the town of Vielsalm in 1976. It took eight years to achieve but it was eventually transported to its present location on February 20, 1984. It's a late 1944 production M4A1(76) VVSS (vertical volute spring suspension) with larger front hull hatches for driver and co-driver and extra armor plates on the hull and turret gun mantle. The new larger Type T23 turret with back ventilator accommodated the M1A2 gun and the barrel was fitted with a factory-installed muzzle brake and there was a new vision cupola for the commander replacing the original rotating hatch ring. It also had the new 'wet' shell storage system in the floor on either side of the main drive. With all these extras it weighed 32.3 tons and was powered by a twin General Motors 6-71 diesel engine giving it a top road speed of almost 30mph with a range of 100 miles and approximately half that for cross-country.

LE CHAR INVINCIBLE
LE COURAGE INVINCIBLE
THE AMERICAN 7th ARMORED DIVISION AND ATTACHED UNITS HEADQUARTERED IN VIELSALM DURING THE CRUCIAL PERIOD OF THE GERMAN OFFENSIVE OF THE ARDENNES IN 1944 HELD THE IMPORTANT CENTER OF ST. VITH PREVENTING ANY ADVANCE AND ANY EXPLOITATION ON THIS MAIN LINE THUS FRUSTRATING THE GERMAN OFFENSIVE BY ITS SACRIFICE PERMITTING THE LAUNCHING OF THE ALLIED COUNTER-OFFENSIVE

ST. VITH, BELGIUM 17-23 DEC. 1944 — DEDICATED 9 JUNE 1984

PRESENTED BY THE SEVENTH ARMORED DIVISION ASSOCIATION IN HONOR OF ALL WHO FOUGHT SO VALIANTLY AT ST. VITH

PARKING
FRITERIE
LE TANK
BRASSERIE
CELLES
ICI FUT ARRETEE
L'OFFENSIVE VON RUNDSTEDT
LE 24 DECEMBRE 1944

PzKpfw V Ausf G Panther Medium Tank

PZKPFW V PANTHER AUSF G

Location: Restaurant "Le Tank," Route d'Achêne, Celles, Belgium
Commemorating: "The end of von Rundstedt's Wacht am Rhein offensive"
Combatants: US Army; German Army
Date: December 24-25, 1944

In the courtyard of the Restaurant "Le Tank" in Celles sits a battle-damaged German Panther, missing its wheels and tracks. A celebratory plaque states that: "Here on 24 December 1944 von Rundstedt's offensive was stopped." The local story is that this tank was the leading Panther of Kampfgruppe Von Cochenhausen, part of 2nd Panzer Division, which was attempting to assault the town of Dinant and secure its bridge over the River Meuse on Christmas Eve 1944. On reaching the crossroads the Germans apparently enquired at the local café whether the road to Dinant was open. Its owner, Marthe Monrique, lied to them, saying it was heavily mined and dangerous, so instead the Germans decided to go through the fields. This lead Panther triggered a mine in the field below the Chateau Acteau and was destroyed. The Germans then halted their advance for a critical amount of time, for on Christmas Day the heavy cloud and winter weather cleared to allow Allied air power to bring the assault to an abrupt halt. The Germans were then finished off by attacks by US 2nd Armored Division supported by British 3RTR. All attempts at relief by Panzer Lehr were defeated and von Cochenhausen and some 600 of his men had to abandon their tanks: they managed to escape on foot. After the war Marthe Monrique rescued the Panther from the field and placed it where it now rests.

Around 400 Panthers were available for the Battle of the Bulge, a few being disguised to look like US M10s and given American camouflage and markings. They were used along with some captured Shermans at the front of some assaults as part of a deception operation to confuse the enemy. It worked—to a point—and a good number of Allied troops were tied down searching for the enemy behind their lines.

Opposite: *Today, a Panther marks the high-water mark of the Battle of the Bulge—or the "von Rundstedt Offensive" as it is signed—in Celles.*

Above Left: *The closest the German attack came to the Meuse was around December 24, when elements of 2nd Panzer Division were about five miles from the Meuse close to Dinant.* NARA

Below Left: *In Foy-Notre Dame, the farthest extent of 2nd Panzer Division's advance is recorded by one of twenty-six battlefield markers erected by the Touring Club de Belgique.*

PANTHER AUSF. G
26/12/1944

PzKpfw V Ausf G Panther Medium Tank

PZKPFW V AUSF G PANTHER

Location: Rue d'Erezée 42, Grandmenil, Belgium
Commemorating: Battle of Grandmenil
Combatants: US Army; German Army
Date: December 24-27, 1944

Near the roundabout on Rue d'Erezée (N807) at the junction with Rue Alphonse Poncelet in Grandmenil sits a German Panther, still with its engine and gearbox, though missing its barrel's muzzle-brake. It bears the number 407 and was part of the 2nd SS-Panzer Division *Das Reich*, having been abandoned when it ran out of petrol during the fierce fighting in this area of the Battle of the Bulge. With the Sixth Panzer Army some five days behind schedule, Hitler ordered *Das Reich* to move south and attempt another breakthrough to take the bridges over the River Meuse. By Christmas Eve 1944 they had almost reached their objective—the bridge at Manhay—attacking the US 75th Infantry Division and the 3rd Armored Division. *Das Reich* initially overwhelmed and broke through the Americans but in the following few days was driven back by a counter-attack combination primarily of artillery and air power, but also armor and infantry.

The Ausf G was the final production model of the Panther and was produced in larger numbers than previous versions, from March 1944 until the end of the war. Ausf G improvements included thicker side armor of 50mm and the modification of the gun mantlet's bottom edge from a circular profile to a wedge shape. This eliminated a lethal weakness in the original curved design of the mantlet that enabled a deliberate frontal shot to deflect straight down through the thin driver's hatch deck armor plating, killing the driver instantly and brewing up the tank. The driver's vision port was also removed in order to strengthen the frontal armor, being replaced with a rotating periscope above the driving position and a new seat was introduced that could be raised to allow the driver's head to emerge from his hatch, allowing for better visibility when not in combat.

Opposite: *7th Armd took positions around Manhay on the 24th. The 2nd SS-Pz Div (Das Reich) attacked late on Christmas Eve. The defenders were deceived by a Judas Goat Sherman leading the enemy column and Manhay was taken. To retake it, 2nd Bn, 424th Inf Regt (of 106th Inf Div) and CCA, 7th Armd, attacked but were badly mauled. In the end, 3rd Bn, 517th PIR retook the village on the 27th.*

Above Left: *A Das Reich Panther destroyed by 3rd Bn, 289th Inf Regt, 75th Inf Div.* NARA

Below Left: *This Panther threw a track reversing toward Manhay.* NARA

M4A1(75) Sherman Medium Tank

Forming part of the Patton Memorial Monument on the outskirts of Ettelbruck, this US M4A1(75) Sherman is a true survivor from the Battle of the Bulge—belonging to the HQ Company of the US 5th Armored Division. It was originally modified to have a bulldozer blade at its front. Although following restoration the blade has been left off, the fittings to attach it remain on the hull glacis plate and the driving train. It also has additional appliqué armor, an M34A1 gun mounting, and an all-round vision cupola for the commander.

Sherman dozers were an invaluable battlefield tool for the Allies. They proved themselves in the landings in Italy and so were in high demand for the Normandy landings and subsequent battles into Germany. They were used in clearing beaches and roadblocks, removing wrecked and damaged vehicles, snow and debris, filling craters, anti-tank ditches, clearing mines, and in building gun emplacements, sand and earth ramps and new approaches to river crossings. The single-section telescopic-jack M1 dozer blade was standardized to fit any Sherman with VVSS suspension, and the later M1A1 blade (14 inches wider) for the HVSS suspension Shermans. Some M4s made especially for the engineering corps had the blades fitted permanently and their turrets removed, otherwise the blades were designed to be removable, either by unbolting or explosive charge.

Ettelbruck had been liberated by the Americans on September 16, 1944, but was retaken by the Germans on December 16. A brief but vicious battle then ensued before Patton's Third Army pushed the Germans back and put an end to their Alzette Valley Offensive by December 25. The American 80th Infantry Division recaptured Ettelbruck after very heavy fighting, and having defeated the German 50th Infantry Division, went on to relieve Bastogne.

M4A1(75) SHERMAN

Location: Patton Monument, 102 Avenue J-F Kennedy, Ettelbruck, Luxembourg
Commemorating: Liberation of Ettelbruck by US Army
Combatants: US Army; German Army
Date: December 27, 1944

Left: *Cult of the personality. The flamboyant General Patton has memorials all over Luxembourg and Belgium. This one is in Ettelbruck near Diekirch. The main square in the town is also named after him and there is a Patton Museum, too—all grist to the tourism mill.*

Right: *The M4A1 is part of the memorial on the outskirts of town. It is in the colors of HQ Company, 34th Tank Battalion, 5th Armored Division, and has the fittings to take a dozer blade.*

Achilles Mk IIC "Northampton" SP Gun

ACHILLES Mk IIC

Location: Rue du Chalet 61, 6980 La Roche-en-Ardenne, Belgium
Commemorating: Liberation of La Roche
Combatants: British Army; German Army
Date: January 11, 1945

Right: *Fireflies of B Squadron East Riding Yeomanry, part of 33rd Armoured Brigade, lining the western bank of the Ourthe in Hotton on January 4. The 33rd Armoured Brigade first supported 53rd Welsh Division, then the advance of the 51st Highland Division.* Battlefield Historian

Opposite: *"Northampton" at La Roche on the River Ourthe. The plaque reads: "Honour and tribute to the 1st Northamptonshire Yeomanry who supported the 51st Highland Division in the liberation of La Roche on 11th January 1945." It is an Achilles, armed with a QF 17pdr in place of the standard 3-inch M7 gun.*

This vehicle—a British Achilles named "Northampton"—is located in the car park opposite the Hôtel du Chalet near the River Ourthe just outside La Roche-en-Ardenne. The plaque on its hull front is dedicated to the 1st Northamptonshire Yeomanry, who supported the 51st Highland Division in this area during Allied counter-attack of the Battle of the Bulge.

The Achilles was the name given by the British to their adaption of the US M10 Woverine tank destroyer. On the point of developing a low-silhouette, self-propelled tank destroyer themselves, they abandoned such plans when the Wolverine became available. The original ones supplied had a US M7 3-inch gun which used a different caliber of ammunition to the Brits, who replaced it with their own successful anti-tank gun, the Ordnance QF 17pdr. Mounted and made mobile, the gun required a distinctive counterweight fitted just behind its muzzle-brake. Rather than use it as the Americans did as a tank hunter, the Brits used their M10s to support infantry and hold ground against German counter-attacks before regular artillery support could be moved up. This maximized the positive aspects of the Achilles—for it was fast and maneuverable over rough ground (20mph) and packed a powerful punch capable of penetrating all but the thickest German armor. However it was thinly armored itself and its turret had an extremely slow manual only rotation which put it at a tactical disadvantage when used offensively. The British also added extra armor plates welded to its front and sides and a top turret shield to improve protection. Some 1,000 Achilles were produced before the end of the war and along with the British Sherman Firefly greatly improved the odds against late-war German heavy armor.

Chapter 5: Operation Dragoon and the Advance to Strasbourg

On August 15, 1944 the Allies began Operation Dragoon—the invasion of southern France. Spearheaded by US VI Corps, the Allied forces included large numbers of French troops in several divisions of French Army B (later designated French First Army, under the command of Général Jean de Lattre de Tassigny), in conjunction with an uprising launched by the French Resistance. The purpose of the operation was to secure the vital ports of Marseille and Toulon on the French Mediterranean coast and so relieve the pressure on the crowded, choked-up ports in Normandy following the D-Day landings. It would also increase the pressure on the German forces in the west by opening up another front.

Though not without its detractors, Dragoon was considered a success, the invasion force of 200,000 men suffering some 12,000 casualties, while the Germans lost 160,000 men—27,000 killed or wounded and 130,000 captured. The operation liberated most of southern France within a month and the port facilities of Marseille and Toulon were reopened by September 20. However, a shortage of fuel then enabled key German units to escape intact, pursued by US 6th Army Group, spearheaded by the French First Army, who forced the Belfort Gap and took Burnhaupt in the Vosges Mountains on November 28. US Seventh Army, including the French 2e DB, forced the Saverne Gap and took Strasbourg on November 23.

Now the only remaining German resistance on the west bank of the Rhine was a pocket centered on and named after the town of Colmar. The final German operation in the West, "Nordwind" (December 31, 1944–January 30, 1945), required German Nineteenth Army to attack out of the pocket in conjunction with Army Group Oberrhein. The thinly stretched US Seventh Army was put under severe pressure, but when reinforcements arrived the attack was soon thwarted. Forced back into the Colmar Pocket, in particularly atrocious winter weather, between January 20 and February 9, 1945, the Nineteenth Army was virtually destroyed as fighting force. Its remnants then retreated, blowing the bridge over the Rhine at Chalampé. The US 6th Army Group was now poised to attack the Siegfried Line.

Previous Page: *It would be mistaken to think that the speed of Seventh Army's advance up the Rhône Valley meant that it was a cakewalk. Here, at Vesovri, two M4s of 756th Tank Battalion (note marking on glacis) have been ambushed and knocked out by German 75mm antitank guns.* NARA

Opposite: *M10 TDs of 191st TD Battalion, 45th Infantry Division ford the Durance River south of Mirabeau.* NARA

Left: *One of a number of PzKpfw V Panthers knocked out during the battle for Meximieux, early September, 1944.* **NARA**

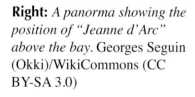

M4A4(75) SHERMAN "JEANNE D'ARC"

Location: 4 Place du Colonel Edon, Marseille, France
Commemorating: The battle for Marseille
Combatants: Free French Army; Germany Army
Date: August 23–28, 1944

M4A4(75) Sherman "Jeanne d'Arc" Medium Tank

"Jeanne d'Arc" bears the insignia of the 2e Régiment de Cuirassier of the 1st French Armored Division (1er DB) and is an original that both participated in and commemorates the fighting for Marseille that took place on August 23–28, 1944. Disabled by a German incendiary grenade, three of its five crew were killed instantly. It was restored and inaugurated as a memorial a year later—on August 25, 1946—and dedicated to the Free French forces who liberated the city.

On August 16 US VI Corps, along with several divisions of the French Army B, supported by a huge naval task force, landed on the beaches of the Côte d'Azur. Opposing them was the German Army Group G, consisting of First Army, Nineteenth Army, and later the Fifth Panzer Army. Made up mainly of wounded veterans and conscripts, it was under strength, badly equipped, and had been severely weakened by the relocation of some of its best divisions to other fronts, leaving only the 11th Panzer Division with any real offensive capability.

Following the Allied landings an insurrection broke out in Marseille on the 20th. The city was surrounded by French General Monsabert commanding French II Corps and 2e Cuirassier launched the first attacks. On the 25th the 1st and 2nd Companies of the 7th Algerian Tirailleurs Regiment, supported by armored vehicles of the 2nd Squadron of the 2e Cuirassiers, stormed the hill of Notre Dame de la Garde. "Jeanne d'Arc" was one of the tanks destroyed during the battle, with its turret crew killed. The ports of Toulon and Marseille were captured in a fortnight and greatly increased the Allied capacity to land men, equipment, fuel, and munitions, giving them a decisive advantage against the Germans.

Right: *A panorma showing the position of "Jeanne d'Arc" above the bay.* Georges Seguin (Okki)/WikiCommons (CC BY-SA 3.0)

Opposite: *"Jeanne d'Arc" was knocked out on August 25 during the liberation of Marseille.* Robert Valette/WikiCommons

A LA MEMOIRE DE L'EQUIPAGE
DU CHAR JEANNE D'ARC
DU 1ERE ESCADRON DU 2EME
REGIMENT DE CUIRASSIERS
TOMBE LE 25 AOUT 1944
POUR LA LIBERATION DE
NOTRE DAME DE LA GARDE
KECK ANDRE MAR. DES LOGIS
GUILLOT ROGER 1ERE CLASSE
CLEMENT MAURICE 2E CLASSE

Libération de Dijon Septembre 1944

Sous-Lieutenant Guérardo, chef de Char
Brigadier-Chef Petithou
Cuirassier Delanatre

Hommage à l'Armée d'Afrique

M4A4(75) Sherman "Duguay-Trouin" Medium Tank

In the little square between the Rue Sambin and Cours Fleury sits the M4A4 Sherman "Duguay-Trouin," an original AFV used by 2e Régiment de Cuirassier (2e RC) of 1er DB, part of the French First Army commanded by Général Jean de Lattre de Tassigny that attacked the Germans at Beaune in the Dijon area on September 6, 1944. Named after a famous French sea captain, "Duguay-Trouin" was the lead tank in a group of five moving east of Meursault when it was hit by two rounds from a German anti-tank weapon from a range of about 3,700ft. One round went through the turret and killed its crew: commander Lieutenant Antoine Cattanéo, gunner Alexis Petitbon, and loader Rene Delaporte. The other tanks in the troop then destroyed the German position. On September 10 at three o'clock in the morning, the first Allied tanks entered the city of Plombières-Lès-Dijon. Then, on the night of September 10–11, a pincer attack forced the

Germans to evacuate Dijon itself. Before leaving, they blew up the station and the Eiffel Bridge to cover their retreat.

French First Army was composed of 82 percent experienced soldiers from units of the Army of Africa (50 percent North Africans, 32 percent Pied-Noirs, 10 percent Black Africans and 8 percent French). In the divisions, the percentage of Maghreb soldiers ranged from 27 percent in 1er DB (armor) to 56 percent in 2nd DIM (Division d'Infanterie Marocaine—Moroccan infantry). By weapon type, this percentage was about 70 percent in the skirmisher regiments, 40 percent in the engineers, and 30 percent in the artillery.

The main determining factor in the success of this southern campaign was the aggressive speed of the Allies, forcing the Germans into reacting to Allied initiatives and making Army Group G fall back and leave Southern France.

M4A4(75) SHERMAN "DUGUAY-TROUIN"

Location: Rue Sambin, Dijon, France
Commemorating: The turret crew of the tank
Combatants: Free French Army; Germany Army
Date: September 6, 1944

Opposite: *"Liberation of Dijon September 1944. This tank "Duguay-Trouin" is of the 2e Regiment of Cuirassiers, which was formed in Oran in 1943 with elements of 2e Regiment de Chasseurs d'Afrique and members of the "Evades de France"* [those who had fled Vichy]. *On September 6, 1944, during the liberation of Dijon, the turret was hit by a German round. Three of the crew were killed: Sublieutenant Gattanéo (tank commander), Corporal Petitbon, and Trooper Delaporte. This honors their sacrifice and those of 40,000 other comrades in arms of the Army of Africa who fell between November 1942 and May 1945. ..."* François de Dijon/WikiCommons (CC BY-SA 3.0)

Left: *Note the Free French diamond marking.*

Location: Rue du Char Champagne, 88270 Ville-sur-Illon, France
Commemorating: Battle of Dompaire
Combatants: Free French Army; Germany Army
Date: September 12–13, 1944

Right and Opposite:
"Champagne" is hidden away in a small village in the Lorraine countryside, but is worth a visit. Note the penetration hole by the engine compartment.

M4A3(76) Sherman "Champagne" Medium Tank

Sitting on a road named after it on the outskirts of Ville-sur-Illo, "Champagne" is another original. It was knocked out during the battle of Dompaire on September 13, 1944. Despite the damage the crew from the 12e Régiment de Chasseurs d'Afrique (RCA), 2e DB, managed to escape without injury.

"Champagne" was fighting as part of the Groupement Tactique Langlade (GTL) under the command of Col Paul Girot de Langlade. This consisted of mechanized infantry from the Régiment de Marche du Tchade and companies from two tank battalions, the 12e RCA and the 501er Régiment de Chars de Combat, along with fighter and artillery support. GTL inflicted a heavy defeat on the recently formed and untested German Panzer-Brigade 112.

On September 12, 1944, the 112th was heading south in two columns. The western column consisted of 1/Panzer-Regiment 29 armed with Panthers, while the eastern column was made up of Panzer-Battalion 2112, armed with PzKpfw IV tanks and the bulk of the armored infantry. They arrived in the area of the French infiltration but failed to detect the French. In the ensuing battle they proved no match for the experienced French colonial troops, who were professional soldiers, hardened in the harsh climate of North Africa and with at least two years of war experience. Although the German tanks outnumbered the French, strength in numbers could not make up for the lack of operational skill in the case of Panzer-Brigade 112, who had made no reconnaissance and lacked of any proper ground or air fire support. The Germans were caught at the bottom of a narrow valley, with the French on three sides supported by fighter bombers and artillery. As a result, in its first engagement Panzer-Brigade 112 had lost 350 dead, and 69 of its 90 tanks.

M8 "Edith" Howitzer Motor Carriage

M8 "EDITH"

Location: 107 Rue de la Division Gén Leclerc, 52700 Andelot-Blancheville, France
Commemorating: 2e DB and the battle of Andelot
Combatants: Free French Army; German Army
Date: September 12, 1944

Located since 2006 in Andelot-Blancheville, "Edith" was hit by a Panzerfaust round that punched a hole in the left side of the hull during the fight for Andelot on September 12, 1944—the day that Général de Lattre's troops from the south joined those of General Leclerc from the north at Nod-sur-Seine. "Edith" is identified with the insignia of the 1er Régiment de Marche des Spahis Marocains, the reconnaissance unit of 2e DB. Spahis were horsemen in the Ottoman army. The French unit dates back to 1914.

The M8, also known as the M8 Scott after US general Winfield Scott), was a self-propelled howitzer developed by the US during World War II using the chassis of the M5 Stuart light tank. It was armed with a 75mm M3 howitzer (based on the M1A1 pack howitzer) in a fully traversable open-topped turret, and carried 46 rounds, the most common types being the M89 white phosphorous shell and the M48 high explosive. It had no coaxial machine gun but there was a .50cal Browning M2HB machine gun mounted on the right rear corner of the turret.

The M8 was manufactured by the Cadillac division of General Motors and a total of 1,778 vehicles was produced from September 1942 until January 1944. It had a crew of four: commander, gunner, driver, and assistant driver/loader. It weighed almost 16 tons and was 16ft 4in long, 7ft 7.5in wide, and 8ft 11in high. It was powered by a Twin Cadillac Series 42 engine which delivered a top road speed of 36mph and a range of 100 miles. M8s saw action in the Italian campaign and also in the Northwest Europe and the Pacific theaters, and it remained in French service after World War II until the 1960s.

Opposite: *"Edith."*

Left: *M8 "Formidable" in summer 1944. The short pack howitzer fitted into an M7 gun mount which made use of components of the M34 gun mount of the M4 medium tank. Extra ammunition was often carried in a trailer towed by the HMC—the Armored Trailer M8—which was manufactured by John Deere— better known for their tractors.* US Army

M4A2(75)
"CORNOUAILLES"

Location: Montée du
Château Milo Gehant,
Belfort, France
Commemorating:
The death of the tank
Commander Lt Martin
Combatants: Free French
Army; German Army
Date: November 21, 1944

Right and Opposite:

*"Cornouailles," one of over
8,000 M4A2s built. Used by
the US Marine Corps, all
others were used for lend-
lease. In British service the
M4A2 armed with the M3 L/40
75mm gun was the Sherman
III; those with the M1A2 L/55
76mm were Sherman IIIAs,
and those Sherman IIIAs with
HVSS became Sherman IIIAYs.
French 2e DB was equipped
with M4A2s.*

M4A2(75) Sherman "Cornouailles" Medium Tank

This M4A2 is named "Cornouailles" (Cornwall) and is sited among the defenses at the Château Milo Gehant in Belfort. It is not an original, but represents a similar Sherman of 6e RCA, 5e DB of the French First Army which was disabled on November 21, 1944, in the Chemin de la Miotte, with its commander Lieutenant Martin killed in the action. The turret of the original is displayed close by.

The old fortified city of Belfort lies just to the north of the Jura and southeast of the Vosges Mountains, controlling the "gateway of Burgundy," a natural route between Alsace and Franche-Comté. Fortified since the Middle Ages, the castle dates to 1226, but the massive fortifications include modifications from the 17th century onward, with Vauban's forts and walls seeing later improvements just before 1940.

In November 1944 the retreating German army managed to hold off the French First Army outside the town until French African Commandos made a successful night attack on the Salbert Fort. Around noon the following day the Sherman tanks of the 6th African Chasseurs Regiment burst through the rue de Cravanche, supported by elements of the 4th Moroccan Regiment. In the northeast, the Commandos de France and the Maquis de Corrèze fought their way through the city and found the main bridges intact thanks to the heroic actions of Edmond Auguié of the FFI (French Forces of the Interior). On the evening of the 20th, only the castle and the forts of Justice, Miotte and Roppe were still holding out. Finally on the 25th around 10:00, a section of the 8th Moroccan Rifle Regiment climbed the walls of the castle and raised the Tricoleur in the citadel for the first time in four years.

M4A3(75)W Sherman "Bourg La Reine" Medium Tank

M4A3(75)W SHERMAN "BOURG LA REINE"

Location: 31 Rue de Nancy, 57370 Phalsbourg, France
Commemorating: Division Leclerc
Combatants: Free French Army; German Army
Date: November 22, 1944

Phalsbourg's military importance is its command of one of the passes through the Vosges Mountains. Its ownership has oscillated throughout its history between Germany (who called it Pfalzburg) and France. On the D604 just outside the town sits the Free French M4A3 Sherman "Bourg La Reine," with a huge hole punched right through its turret by a deadly 88mm round. This tank is an original, destroyed on November 22, 1944, on this spot during the liberation of the town by Division Leclerc.

One of the most famous tanks of the third squadron, 12th Cuirassier Regiment of the 2e DB, much is known about "Bourg La Reine's" demise. The first shell killed the driver and a second round struck the turret ring, putting it out of action and causing the rest of the crew to bail out, just as a third shell penetrated the fuel tank and set the vehicle on fire. The halftrack which raced to help was also hit and set on fire, killing its female driver and injuring the rest of the escaped crew of "Bourg La Reine."

After the battle the tank was preserved at the behest of General Leclerc and erected as a monument by the municipality of Phalsbourg in tribute to the liberators. Confusingly, there is another Sherman with the same name also serving as a monument in Bourg la Reine itself, however it is a replica.

This M4A3(75)W is equipped with an M3 75mm gun, large hull hatches, a 47° glacis, and wet ammunition stowage bins. Dubbed the Sherman IV by the British, it had a welded hull with a sloping rear plate, was powered by a Ford GAA 8-cylinder liquid-cooled engine with a top speed of 26mph and a range of 100 miles. It had VVSS suspension.

Opposite: *The tank today. Note the two impact holes on turret and side.*

Left: *It was as the division forced the Saverne Gap toward Strasbourg that "Bourg La Reine" met its fate. It was photographed a few days after it was destroyed—the hole in the turret is unmistakeable. The French did not officially receive any M4A3(75)Ws by Lend Lease, but they were provided with many different types of Shermans from US reserves in order to make up for losses.* NARA

M10 Wolverine "Porc-Epic" Tank Destroyer

Situated on the outskirts of Illhausen on the D106 going towards Elsenheim is the M10 Wolverine Tank destroyer "Porc-Epic" (porcupine), knocked out by a German Nashorn of Kampfgruppe Blasius at this location on January 26, 1945, during the battle of the Colmar Pocket. The monument commemorates the 121 fallen of the 8e Régiment de Chasseurs d'Afrique (8RCA) and the crew members of 8RCA M10s who died in the battle—three from "Porc-Epic," two from "Crotale IV" (rattlesnake) and one from "Margouillat III" (a Saharan lizard).

8RCA had been temporarily attached to the 1er DFL (Free French Division), commanded by Général Pierre Garby to liberate the Colmar Pocket. Facing them were four battalions of the 708th Volksgrenadier Division supported by Nashorn tank destroyers and heavy artillery. The Germans were positioned in deep defense lines using the small villages and woods to control the wide open spaces in front of them, which they had also mined. A German spoiling counter-attack was repulsed and on January 26–27 1st Brigade of 8RCA concentrated on circumventing Elsenheim woods which were assaulted by 3e Batallion de la Légion Etrangère (the French Foreign Legion). On January 28 the village of Grussenheim was liberated with support of the tanks of the 2e DB but the French incurred heavy losses. Slowly the attack continued and German defense was worn down, until on January 31 the villages of Elsenheim and Markolsheim were liberated and the French forces finally reached the River Rhine on the following day.

Although known as tank destroyers, M10s were drawn increasingly into infantry support roles that exposed them to artillery and infantry fire, so their crews took to piling up sandbags to detonate Panzerfaust rockets before they reached the thin armor and turret tops were also improvised. Some 200 Wolverines served in the Free French Army, where they were popular.

M10 WOLVERINE "PORC-EPIC"

Location: D106 Illhaeusern, 68970 France
Commemorating: The fallen of 8RCA
Combatants: Free French Army; German Army
Date: End of January 1945

Opposite: *"Porc-Epic" and the 8RCA memorial. Three members of its crew, whose Claude Beaufils, René Cardot and René Garnier, were killed during this action. The commander, Marc Samin, survived. In his Osprey book on the M10 Steven Zaloga identifies 47 of the 227 M10s allocated to French regiments were lost in combat, with either 2e DB or French First Army.* Gzen92/WikiCommons (CC BY-SA 4.0)

Left: *To the north, in Chavannes-les-Grands, there is a memorial to the 1er Regiment de Chasseurs d'Afrique in the form of M4A4(75) Sherman "Foch."* Rauenstein/WikiCommons (CC BY-SA 3.0)

Location: 2 rue de la Première Armée Francaise, 68000 Colmar, France
Commemorating: 5e DB's liberation of Colmar
Combatants: Free French Army; German Army
Date: February 2, 1945

Right: *There are two plaques associated with this tank: the first remembers the liberation of Colmar. The other, the Polish soldiers who died in Alsace during the war. The latter, unveiled in May 1980, "on the occasion of the 35th anniversary of the victory over Hiler's fascism."*

Far Right and Opposite:
The tank today in a park in Colmar. Note the suspension, the late war HVSS. Poudou99/ aka Kootshisme/WikiCommons (CC BY-SA 3.0)

M4A1E8(76) HVSS Sherman Medium Tank

On the corner of rue de la Première Armée Francaise and rue de la Cavalerie sits this Free French M4A1E8(76) HVSS Sherman commemorating the liberation of the town by 5e DB on February 2 1945. The Germans defended the areas of Alsace and Lorraine staunchly, as they considered them part of Germany and they created a buffer between the French and the Rhine; the French themselves saw the Rhine as the boundary.

By November 1944 German forces west of the Rhine were reduced to a 40 x 30-mile pocket centered on the town of Colmar and thus named after it. In a bitter fight that raged from November 1944 to February 1945 which devastated the entire Alsace plain and its foothills, 295,000 French and 125,000 American troops of the US Sixth Army Group fought the German Nineteenth Army. The forces from Sixth Army Group eventually consisted of US 3rd, 28th, and 75th Infantry and 12th Armored divisions, along with French First Army's divisions (three armored—1er, 2e, and 5e— and six infantry (1er DFI, 2e (Moroccan), 3e (Algerian), 4e (Moroccan Mountain), 9th (Colonial), 10e) plus a number of smaller units such as paratroopers. The French lost some 14,000 men and the Americans about 6,500. The Germans were decisively beaten and lost over 20,000 men, but were still able to evacuate 50,000 troops and much materiel.

Manufactured exclusively by the Pittsburg Pressed Steel Car Company, the M4A1(76)W was also known as the M4A1E8 (Easy Eight)—a reference to the number of bogies it used with the new HVSS which enabled the tank to have wider tracks (23 inches instead of 16) giving it better cross-country performance. Powered by Continental R975 C1 9-cylinder radial petrol engine it had a top road speed of 25mph and an operational range of 120 miles.

M4A1(75)s of Combat Command B, 13th Armored Regiment, US 1st Armored Division, moving toward their bivouac area, Anzio, April 27, 1944. Note the size of the .50cal Browning M2HB AAMG and 1A-13A markings on rear of last tank. NARA

Chapter 6: The Soft Underbelly

Following the first victory over Axis forces in North Africa, there was fierce debate between the Allies as to what to do next. The British favored crossing the Mediterranean to invade Sicily, then Italy, in a peripheral approach where they could bring their superior naval power to bear, while the Americans took a more direct approach, arguing for a full-scale invasion of France. In the end the compromise included both, with the main effort concentrated on Normandy set for 1944, while a smaller Italian campaign was begun immediately, first with the invasion of Sicily (Operation Husky) July 9, 1943, and then invasion of Italy September 9, 1943 (Operations Avalanche, Baytown, and Slapstick). The troops assembled for the invasion of Italy were probably the most international of all Allied forces—British and Commonwealth, American, Canadian, Free French, South African, Polish, Australian, Brazilian, New Zealand, Greek, Belgian, Czechoslovakian as well as some Italian royalists and partisans.

Facing them was German Army Group C. What followed was a steep learning curve for the Allies, and Italy certainly proved no "soft underbelly"—as Winston Churchill had hoped. For almost two years from July 10, 1943—May 2, 1945, in the beach landings, bridgeheads, and eventual breakouts to the painfully slow progress up through the Italian mainland, no other campaign in the Western theater was so costly to both sides.

Italy's terrain, crisscrossed with mountain ranges, favored the defender—a role in which the Wehrmacht excelled. After the successful Allied landings in Salerno and the not so successful one at Anzio, the Germans fought a series of stubborn rearguard actions based around a series of cleverly constructed defensive lines: the Winter Line, consisting of the Gustav Line from the Garigliano to Sangro rivers, anchored on Monte Cassino and including the subsidiary Hitler and Bernhardt Lines; the Caesar Line guarding Rome, and the final Gothic Line, a string of heavily fortified positions north of Florence.

The Allied forces eventually numbered 1,334,000 fighting 500,000 Axis troops. Both sides would lose over 335,000 men apiece by the end of the campaign, which didn't end until a week before the unconditional surrender of May 7, 1945.

Opposite: *An unusual sight—an M26 Pershing, the US heavy tank that saw limited action at the end of the war, in Brescello. It has seen some changes: the barrel and mantlet are from an M47. Brescello is where Giovannino Guareschi's Don Camillo was brought to life in a series of movies. In one of them an M24 Chaffee is used to represent a German tank, but when the town tried to get one they ended up with an M26 instead. The Don Camillo and Peppone Museum is in the same square.* Itto Ogami/WikiC (CC BY 3.0)

Left: *The "Green Books," the series of official histories produced by the US Army after the war, are the first port of call for anyone who wants to read about the American view of World War II. They have extensive mapping such as this showing the stalemate of Spring 1944 with the Allies clinging on to their Anzio bridgehead while being stymied by the defenses of the Gustav line and Monte Cassino.* Center of Military History, US Army

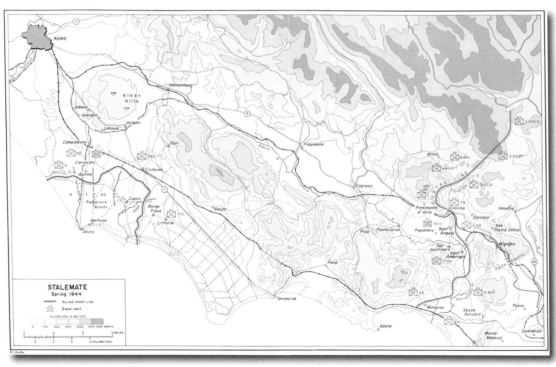

STALEMATE
Spring 1944

23319

RE 281022

AI
CADUTI DI MARSALA
I CARRISTI D'ITALIA

Semovente M41 da 75/34 Self-Propelled Gun

SEMOVENTE M41 DA 75/34

Location: Piazza Guglielmo Marconi, 91025 Marsala, Sicily
Commemorating: The fallen of Marsala
Combatants: Italian Army; Allied Armies
Date: July–August 1943

This Italian Semovente M41 da 75/34 in Marsala is dedicated by the tank men of Italy. Operation Husky, the Allied invasion of Sicily, was a short but hard-fought affair that began on July 9 and ended on August 17, 1943. The island was seen by the Allies as an essential stepping-stone for the invasion of the Italian mainland and Hitler ordered that it must be held at all costs, so German strength was initially increased, but with overwhelming Allied air superiority and coastal defenses manned by increasingly unwilling Italians the Allied landings could not be stopped. In three days the British cleared the southeast while the Americans moved west. Marsala, on the northwest tip of the island, was heavily bombed by several hundred US planes and fell to US 3rd Division on July 24. That same day Mussolini was voted down in Rome and resigned. The new government entered into peace negotiations with the Allies prompting the German commander, Field Marshal Albert Kesselring, to remove all German troops from the island. The night of August 11–12 saw a well-executed withdrawal of 40,000 German and 60,000 Italian troops to the mainland, almost under the noses of the Allies, rendering all the posturing of the Allied commanders—Patton and Montgomery—something of a side issue.

The Semovente series was mostly used as mobile artillery at divisional level, but also had tank-killing capability and they performed well early in the war in the deserts of North Africa. Although mounting the powerful 75/18 gun they were made with riveted and bolted armor plates that were considerably weaker than welded or cast armor, and its equally old-fashioned 1930s-style suspension did not allow for great speed. It also lacked a machine gun for self protection and as a result proved vulnerable to infantry assaults. The last Semoventes saw action in north Italy and the Balkans in German hands.

Opposite: *Monument given to the city of Marsala by the Association of Carristi (tankmen) of Italy in memory of the Allied carpet-bombing of the city on May 11, 1943.* Otrebla86/WikiCommons

Left: *The heavier Semovente 105/25 "Bassotto" was Italy's most powerful self-propelled gun and the Germans made use of it—as StuG M43 mit 105/25 853 (i)—after the Italian surrender.* George Forty Collection

M4(75) Sherman Medium Tank

Right: *Should the Allies have bombed the monastery or not? US 36th Inf Div CG Gen Walker didn't think so: "This was a valuable historical monument, which should have been preserved. The Germans were not using it and I can see no advantage in destroying it. No tactical advantage will result since the Germans can make as much use of the rubble for observation posts and gun positions as of the building itself." This is exactly what happened following the abbey's destruction.*

Opposite: *M4 at the small museum near the Italian cemetery Mignano Montelungo.* edella/Shutterstock

In the Piazza Alcide De Gasperi in Cassino sits a rusty US M4 Sherman bearing no discernible insignia. Monte Cassino in the Apennine Mountains has a historic hilltop abbey that towers above the nearby town of Cassino, guarding the entrances to the Liri and Rapido valleys. It was part of the German defense known as the Gustav Line which was in turn part of the in-depth defenses of the Winter Line. This was the strategic point for the Allied forces to break through those defenses and take Rome.

In a savage series of battles that lasted from mid-January to mid-May 1944, four separate Allied assaults were launched against Monte Cassino using troops from all the Allied armies. The first battle took place in January 1944 and was led by a US Army thrust with armored regiments. This incurred heavy losses (such as this M4) in the closed and wooded steep terrain that favored the defenders. From their eyrie at the top the Germans could see anything going on and respond accordingly. Their defense was tenacious. The second offensive in mid-February again failed and resulted in one of the most hotly debated incidents of the war when the abbey was obliterated by Allied bombers. The Germans then occupied the rubble and established yet more excellent defensive positions.

The third battle of Cassino in mid-March was preceded by a colossal artillery barrage from 900 guns and a massive aerial bombardment of the town, but the follow-up ground attacks by New Zealand troops once again ended in failure. Only with the launch of Operation Diadem in May 1944 did the Gustav Line finally collapse when II Polish Corps succeeded in capturing the abbey on May 18, thus ending one of the longest and bloodiest engagements of the Italian campaign. The total Allied casualties numbered 55,000 compared to 20,000 German, along with an unknown number of civilians.

M4A2(75) Sherman Medium Tank

Location: Near Albaneta Farm, Monte Cassino, Italy
Commemorating: 4th Polish Armoured Regiment
Combatants: Allied Forces including Polish units; German Army
Date: May 12, 1944

Right: *The memorial— designed by artist and sculptor Lt Władysław Kuźniarz—was unveiled on May 18, 1946. Note the scorpions that have since been stolen.* Photos: National Digital Archives, Poland

Opposite: *There are two plaques on the memorial. This one reads: "It was here that, on 12 May 1944, the first soldiers of the armoured forces newly formed in the east, fell in battle. 2Lt Białecki, Ludomir Cpl Ambroźej, Edward Cpl Bogdajewicz, Eugeniusz Cpl Karcewicz, Bolesław Cpl Nieckowski, Józef." It goes on to list other losses. The other side says, "Heroes of the 4th Armoured Regiment who gave their lives marching to Poland."* Photos courtesy www.irish brigade.co.uk

Near the remains of the medieval Albaneta Farm complex, below Hill 593 and behind the Polish cemetery at Monte Cassino, stands a memorial to the "Skorpions," the Polish 4th Armoured Regiment, and to the crew of the Sherman whose carcass forms the basis for the monument. 2Lt Ludomir Białecki's tank struck a mine on May 12, 1944, during the first Polish assault on Monte Cassino monastery.

On September 1, 1939, Germany invaded Poland and 16 days later Germany's ally, the Soviet Union, invaded from the east. As the country was dismembered, those Polish officers and men who did not die in battle—or were murdered by Stalin—were sent into camps in the Soviet Union.

When Germany turned on its ally in 1941 and the Soviets joined the alliance against Hitler, the Polish government in exile negotiated to have its countrymen freed to form an army. When agreement was reached, Major General Wladislaw Anders became its commander, and at the Quebec conference in August 1943 Churchill decided to send II Polish Corps to Italy. After training in Palestine, the understrength corps—the Poles always suffered from manpower shortages, especially replacements for battle casualties—left Alexandria for Italy on April 4, 1943. 4th Armoured Regiment was equipped with 52 Sherman IIIs (M4A2) and 11 Stuart Vs (M3A3).

The Poles arrived as the Allies were assaulting the Gustav Line, the lynchpin of which was Monte Cassino. It had withstood three assaults already: the Poles' attack would be the fourth. The offensive started on the night of May 11/12 and was beaten back by German artillery; during the day Point 593 (Mt Calvary) and Albaneta Farm were taken, but the Poles were forced back by German counterattacks. Further attacks were made on May 13, 14, and 16 before the 12th Podolski Lancers hoisted the Polish flag over the monastery on the 18th.

Sturmgeschütz III Ausf G Assault Gun

STURMGESCHÜTZ III AUSF G

Location: Garibaldi Square, Castiglion Fiorentino, Italy
Commemorating: All fallen tank crew of all wars
Combatants: Multinational Allied Forces; German Army
Date: May 1944

This German StuG III Ausf G is part original (the lower chassis and running gear) and part replica (the engine decking, fenders, fighting compartment and gun barrel). It was abandoned by the Germans when it collapsed a local bridge and was buried in the ruins until recovered and restored in 1990 by a local tank association. It was painted in an approximately accurate camouflage of green stripes over desert sand and inaugurated on May 30, 1993.

The StuG III Ausf G was the final model of the series, produced in vast numbers (almost 8,000) from December 1942 onward until the end of the war in March 1945. It was based on the chassis of the PzKpfw III with a turretless armored superstructure housing a more powerful gun. The main difference between it and previous versions was the new superstructure with its slanted sides overlapping the top of the tracks, made up of 30mm armor with 50mm plates at the front. Another Ausf G modification was to the roof hatches, with the introduction of a commander's cupola, fitted with seven periscopes and an SE14Z scissors periscope that could be raised through a hinged port in the forward edge of the hatch lid. The roof hatch for the gunner was then removed and replaced with a periscope sight. The vehicle weighed 23.9 tons, had a crew of four and was powered by a 320hp Maybach HL120TRM V-12 engine giving it a top speed of 25mph and a range of 100 miles. Its main armament was the 7.5cm StuK40 L/48—the most numerous anti-tank gun used by the German army. Originally conceived as an infantry support weapon the StuG III morphed into its anti-tank role as Germany was increasingly forced onto the defensive.

Opposite: *This StuG III has been heavily restored.* Stefanomencarelli WikiCommons

Left: *This StuG III of StuG-Brigade 907 was knocked out near Aquino by the British 64th Anti-tank Regiment. StuG-Brigade 907 was formed in Schweinfurt in January 1944, being equipped with its StuGs at Ferentino after transfer to Italy. It was immediately sent into action at Anzio as part of German Tenth Army before moving to the Monte Cassino area in May 1944.* George Forty Collection

Above Right: *On July 21, 2016, a large bronze sculpture, "Peace Through Valour," was unveiled in Toronto's Nathan Phillips Square's Sculpture Court. It remembered more than 93,000 Canadians who fought in Italy. It depicts a topographical map of Ortona illustrating the destruction the town endured. Each corner is guarded by Canadian soldiers standing vigil. Sculptor Lum took inspiration from photographs and paintings by Canadian artist Charles Comfort. Lum said the model is meant to be looked at with downcast eyes and is scaled to be engaging to people of all ages—particularly children from the nearby playground.*
Courtesy of the artist Ken Lum

M4(75) Sherman "Athena"/"Cookie" Medium Tank

Forming part of the Price of Peace Monument in Ortona, this M4(75) Sherman bears two names along with both US and Canadian markings and a rather confusing back story. Now it commemorates the battle of Ortona. During late December 1944 soldiers of the 1st Canadian Infantry Division fought a savage battle to dislodge Germany's battle-hardened 1st Fallschirmjäger Division from the town—the culmination of the fighting on the Adriatic front in Italy.

However, it turns out that this tank was originally called "Cookie." It was an early production M4 made by the American Locomotive Company and later retrofitted with appliqué armor on its hull and turret. It served with Task Force Brown of CCA, US 7th Armored Division, in September 1944 in the Overloon area of the Netherlands—over 800 miles away! In the early hours of the assault on the German fortifications near Overloon it overturned in a ditch and was abandoned by its crew.

It ended up in the collection of the Dutch War and Resistance Museum at Overloon until it was sold to a group of Canadians looking for a Sherman to commemorate the battle of Ortona. It was then modified with some Canadian insignia, the numbering (174) of the Three Rivers Regiment, 1st Canadian Armoured Brigade, which landed with the 1st Canadian Division on the beaches of Sicily and supported them all the way to Ortona. It was presented to the town on July 31, 2006. The plaque on the left side of the hull reads: "This tank honours veterans of the 12th Canadian Armoured Regiment (TRR) and Sergeant Rudy Vinet, 27th Anti-Tank Battery (RCA) and is donated to the citizens of Ortona through the generosity of Seymour Schulich, CM, Harry Steel, OC, Michael Wekerle, and John Cleghorn, OC."

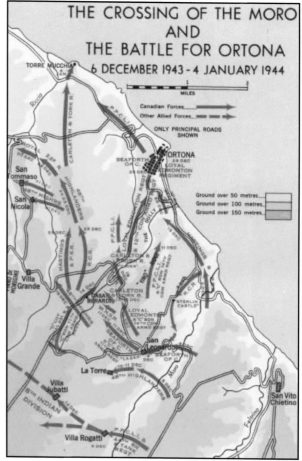

Above Left and Left: *"Athena" in Ortona.* Both: Ra Boe (CC BY-SA 2.5)

Above: *Map of the advance on Ortona. Canadian Official*

Opposite, Below: *The memorial for Canadian soldiers who died in Ortona.* Ra Boe (CC BY-SA 2.5)

The Semovente M42 da 75/18 was titled the Sturmgeschütz M42 mit 75/18 850(i) in German service. Vitold Muratov Wiki/(CC BY-SA 3.0)

Semovente M42 da 75/18 Assault Gun

SEMOVENTE M42 DA 75/18

Location: Parco Fauna Orobica, Bergamo, Italy
Commemorating: Italian tankmen of WWII
Combatants: Italian Army; Allied Armies
Date: 1959

This Italian Semovente M42 da 75/18 bears the ram's head insignia of the Ariete Armored Division painted on the left side of the superstructure and a plate that states that it is "A gift of the tankers of Bergamo to the city." It has been on display in the open since 1959 but with a fake wooden gun. After a partial restoration by OTO Melara in 2007, in which the fake gun was replaced with a more correct replica, a canopy was installed over it to give more protection from the elements.

The Semovente series was inspired by the German Sturmgeschütz III, designed by an Italian artillery colonel, Sergio Berlese, and constructed by Fiat Ansaldo. There were three versions, each consecutively based on the M13/40, M14/41, and M15/42 tank chassis and their respective engines. The first (M13/40) was produced in 1941 and used successfully in North Africa in 1942. The second, based on the M14/41, was produced from 1941 to 1943, and the third on the M15/42 from 1943 until the Italian surrender and beyond by the Germans, who seized 130 Semoventes for their own use and forced the continued production of another 55.

The Semovente M42 da 75/18 had thicker armor (50mm), used spring leaf suspension and the Fiat-SPA 15TB diesel engine that gave it a top speed of 20mph. The gun was based on the 75mm Obice da 75/18 modello 34 mountain gun—also designed by Col Sergio Berlese. It protruded through a half-ball mantlet that allowed a traverse and elevation of 40° and was fitted with a muzzle-break punctured with distinctive small circular blast holes. The Semoventes were meant for infantry support and indirect fire, but their low

silhouette and powerful gun, capable of firing HE, AP, or HEAT shells, meant they also performed well in an anti-tank role.

Left: *The Ariete Division's ram's head insignia.*

Below: *Extra frontal protection for this Semovente M42, seen in the north African desert.*

M36 Gun Motor Carriage

M36

Location: War Memorial
Viale Monumento
Municipio, 82010 Arpaise,
Italy
Commemorating: Those
locals from Arpaise who
died in WWII
Combatants: US Army;
German Army
Date: 1944

Right: *The open turret of the M36 must have been cold during the battles in the Ardennes in 1944-45. Although postwar the US Army decided that the concept of tank destroyers had not worked, the crews liked the M36 and by the end of the war it had killed a lot of German tanks, and had proved especially useful against pill-boxes and bunkers.*

Opposite: *The speed of the M36 often got it out of trouble when faced by heavier opponents. It proved to be a potent weapon and was the standard US tank destroyer in late 1944–1945. The M36 was used by the Italian Army postwar.* Corrado Marra

Mounted on a stone ramp in the center of the town's war memorial beneath a giant "A," this M36 is open to the elements, looking unloved, and rusting away. Although the gun and its shield are replicas, its serial number of 8624 shows it as an M10A1 built by Fisher in January, 1944, and converted that same year to an M36 by the Commerce International Co.

The M10/M10A1 (the former based on the M4A2 chassis; the latter the M4A3) tank destroyers had been armed with the M7 3-inch gun with scanty armor protection and a top speed of around 30mph. Some 7,000 were built, a number being converted to M35 prime movers towing such heavy weapons as the 240mm gun, and a number being completed with the new M36 turret.

In October 1942, realizing that harder hitting power was needed to combat the later German tanks, trials started to adapt a 90mm anti-aircraft gun for use with the M10. Immediately it became obvious that the turret wouldn't work, and so a new one was designed. It needed a significant counterweight to balance the heft of the M3 gun, but the results were good and conversion of M10 and M10A1 vehicles began immediately. 1,298 of the standard M36 were produced or converted, 187 of the M36B1 (M4A3), and 287 of the M36B2 (M4A2). The latter saw the introduction of a set of folding panels to enclose the top of the turret and protect the crew from shrapnel.

The M36 first saw action in Europe in October 1944 and would prove to be an excellent weapon—as was proved by its longevity as it saw action postwar into the 1950s, the Italian Army using the M36 into the 1960s. Replacing both towed anti-tank guns and the earlier M10 tank destroyer, the M36's M3 90mm gun was effective against all but the Tiger's frontal armour and gave the US Army a weapon similar to the British Sherman Firefly.

Chapter 7: Russia and East Europe

The battles of World War II on the Eastern Front are the largest military confrontations in history, fought with such ferocity that they account for almost half the total deaths of the war: over 30,000,000 people, many of them civilians. On June 22, 1941, Hitler launched Operation Barbarossa in a bid to seize German *Lebensraum* (living space) and destroy the "Jewish Bolshevik" Russian state. His dehumanization of Slavic and Jewish peoples enabled a savage program of death doled out on an industrial scale. However, the euphoria of initial victories and fast progress evaporated as the Nazis could not take Moscow but instead were pushed back and drawn into increasingly desperate war of attrition, to eventually be worn down by the seemingly endless reserves that the USSR could produce to replace whole armies that it lost.

Over almost four years, June 22, 1941–May 25, 1945, a series of titanic battles were fought. The battle of Moscow (October 2, 1941–January 7, 1942) involved some 3,500,000 combatants and 6,000 tanks, with the Russians losing over a million men and the Germans 200,000. The siege of Leningrad (September 8, 1941–January 27, 1944) involved 1,600,000 combatants and resulted in over a million Soviets and 580,000 German deaths. Perhaps the most bloody of all was the battle of Stalingrad (August 23, 1942–February 2, 1943) involving over 2,200,000 men, the Russians suffering 1,130,000 casualties and the Germans 768,380. Next the battle of Kursk (July 5, 1943–August 23, 1943) involving nearly 3,000,000 men and 8,000 tanks and resulting in over 5,000,000 casualties. Finally the battle of Berlin (April 16–May 2, 1945) had over 3,500,000 combatants and resulted in over 200,000 casualties.

Previous Page: *The liberation of Kyiv (Kiev) on November 5, 1943, is remembered in this monument near the Shulyavska metro station on Peremohy Avenue, Kyiv. Behind, the panels that make up the Alley of the the Hero Cities of the Soviet Union. Brest Fortress and 12 cities were awarded this title for heroism during World War II: Kerch, Kyiv, Leningrad, Minsk, Moscow, Murmansk, Novorossiysk, Odessa, Sevastopol, Smolensk, Stalingrad, Tula.* Ferran Cornellà/WikiCommons (CC BY-SA 3.0)

Opposite: *Russian Su-85 SP guns move through the streets of Berlin.* George Forty Collection

Left: *T-34 tanks and crews in training on the Eastern Front, 1942. The T-34 crewman had to be small as the turret was small. It also lacked a turret basket.* George Forty Collection

Sturmgeschütz III Ausf D Assault Gun

Location: Volokolamsk, Russia
Commemorating: The battle of Moscow
Combatants: German Army; Red Army
Date: October 1941– January 1942

Right and Opposite: *The defense of Moscow is justly remembered by a number of memorials, but none are more remarkable than the two linked to the 8th Guards Panfilov Division—the one illustrated and the Twenty-Eight Guards-men Memorial at Dubosekov three miles away. This memorial to the engineers who contributed to the defense, particularly the squad led by P.I. Firstov and his political director A.M. Pavlov. Formed from the 316th Rifle Division, the 8th Guards was named after its commander and posthumous Hero of the Soviet Union, Ivan Vasilyevich Panfilov.*
Both: 3BYK BETPA/Wi-kiCommons (CC BY-SA 4.0)

Just to the east of the Russian city of Volokolamsk, 75 miles west of Moscow, a monument representing a German Sturmgeschütz III hitting a mine—the silver metal shards—is a memorial to the battle for the Soviet capital. Had the Russians lost, and Moscow fallen, the course of the war may have been very different.

This StuG III is a rare Ausf D version recovered from the battlefield and restored, before being incorporated into this memorial, dedicated to the 11 Red Army engineers who managed to hold up the German advance in this vicinity on November 18, 1941. At some point the StuG was looted for parts but it was restored in 2010–2011.

The StuG III was envisaged as an assault artillery infantry support weapon—*Sturmartillerie*—that was not used for indirect fire but rather for direct line-of-sight fire at targets within three miles, using HE shells. 150 Ausf Ds were produced May–September 1941, replacing losses sustained during Operation Barbarossa, and some were modified into command vehicles.

The StuGs used faced-hardened armor—as was the case on all German front and side hull plates at the time: a very thin layer of brittle, hard steel backed by ductile, non-brittle armor that absorbed impact and supported the hard layer. The hardened layer was supposed to break the incoming projectile's nose—even rounds with armor-piercing caps. Such face-hardening had mixed results and stopped in mid-1944. It was not used on later German heavy tanks; with their thicker armor and long-range main guns it was not deemed necessary—or perhaps it reflects a decline in the quality of German manufacturing capability at this stage of WWII.

Panzerbefehlswagen III Ausf F Command Tank

PANZERBEFEHLS-WAGEN III AUSF F

Location: Buinichi Field Memorial, Bunichevo Park, Mogilev, Belarus
Commemorating: The defenders of Mogliev
Combatants: German Army; Red Army
Date: July 1941–June 1944

In Bunichevo Park, Mogilev, there is a memorial complex to the defenders of the city in WWII, which includes Russian artillery and an IS-2, a chapel, a memorial to the 172nd Infantry Division, and a Panzerbefehlswagen III that was fished out of a river. Mogilev held out for 23 days in July 1941 before it was occupied by the Nazis and was completely devastated in the fighting. It had held the Germans away from Smolensk and given time for Field Marshal Semyon Timoshenko to bring in reinforcements. The delay to the Germans at Mogilev and Smolensk contributed materiually towards the defense of Moscow.

Belarus was subjected to a terrifying regime of ethnic cleansing to make way for German colonization and lost a quarter of its prewar population. Mogilev was liberated on June 28, 1944, and German troops were finally expelled from the country in August 1944 with the completion of the colossal Soviet Operation Bagration—a series of battles involving over two million men and thousands of AFVs.

The Panzerbefehlswagen was a command version of the PzKpfw III, giving unit commanders mobility and communications on the battlefield. The Germans had a high proportion of command tanks something that gave them a distinct tactical advantage. Under 50 vehicles of each of the first versions (Ausf D1 and Ausf E) were built. They had a dummy gun in a turret, more vision ports, an extra long-range radio set with a distinctive curved frame antenna, and only an exterior-mounted machine gun for defense. The first to be mass-produced, the Ausf H, continued with the mock turret and dummy gun, but the next model—the Aus J—was the first in the series to retain the PzKpfw III's main gun (a short-barrelled 5cm KwK38). The Ausf K was an upgrade to the long-barrelled 5cm KwK39 L/60 main gun and also a change of antenna from the distinctive bent loop to a more discreet star version. This was the last model produced.

Opposite and Above Left:
The main gun and mantlet are fake, but the ball-mounted coaxial MG was real. Alkhimov Maxim/ WikiCommons (CC BY 3.0); Futureal/WikiCommons (CC BY-SA 3.0)

Left: *The defense of Mogilev as the German Panzers close in. The main body of defenders was a mixture of 110th and 172nd Infantry Divisions with remnants from a number of other units under General Mikhail Romanov who was captured at the last when his troops tried to break out.* Alkhimov Maxim/ WikiCommons (CC BY 3.0)

T-34/85, IS-2, IS-3, SU-100, ISU-152, and BM-13

T-34/85, IS-2, IS-3, SU-100, ISU-152 AND BM-13

Location: Prokhorovka Memorial, Belgorod oblast, near Kursk, Russia
Combatants: Red Army; German Army
Commemorating: Battle of Prokhorovka (and the battle of Kursk)
Date: July 12, 1943

Close to the imposing central 170ft high memorial bell tower built as a centerpiece in 1995 in the Parkovaya Ulitsa of Prokhorovka is a display of Soviet tanks and SP artillery including many of the types that fought in the fierce battle here on July 12, 1943, part of the larger battle of Kursk that took place between July 5 and August 23 that year. Kursk, famous as the biggest tank engagement in history, was the German Army's Operation Zitadelle (Citadel), an attempt to pinch off the salient created by the Soviet victory at Stalingrad.

Forewarned by British enigma decryptions—and, possibly, by their own cryptanalysis from captured machines—the Soviets were able to construct a series of deep defensive lines bristling with anti-tank guns, artillery, minefields and anti-tank ditches upon which the German attacks were eventually broken. The Russians then launched their own counteroffensives. The Battle of Prokhorovka started with the Soviet 5th Guards Tank Army's counter thrust (Operation Kutuzov) against SS-Obergruppenführer und General der Waffen-SS Paul Hausser's II SS-Panzer Corps (three Waffen-SS Panzer divisions: 1st *Leibstandarte*, 2nd *Das Reich*, and 3rd *Totenkopf)*.

Until recently, it was believed that 5th Guards suffered massive losses of 300–400 tanks in their heroic counterattacks as they succeeded in preventing the Germans from capturing Prokhorovka and breaking through their third and final heavily fortified line. Recent analysis, however, has called into question the actual number of tanks involved at Kursk in general, and Prokhorovka specifically.

Whatever the truth of this, there's no debate about the fact that the two German attacks were defeated, the Wehrmacht called off Operation Zitadelle, and the Red Army launched their own Operation Polkovodets Rumyantsev in the south while continuing with Operation Kutuzov in the north. In this way the Soviets were able to seize the strategic initiative on the Eastern Front, which it held for the rest of the war. After the war, the Prokhorovka battlefield was enshrined as a memorial to Soviet resistance.

Opposite:
Above Left: *SU-100 with the slogan "We're from Uralmash!" (a tank assembly plant) and T-34/85s.* Navigator-avia/WikiCommons (CC BY 2.0)

Above Right: *ISU-152 and IS-2s.* Alexander Kochanov/ WikiCommons (CC BY 3.0)

Below: *ISU-152 (slogan "Death to the Fascist beast!") and IS-3.* Alexander Persona Grata/WikiCommons (CC BY 2.0)

Left: *The bell tower on Prokhorovka Field.* Voyagerim/WikiCommons (CC BY 2.0)

IS-2 M1943 with M1944 Turret Heavy Tank

Location: Izyum, Kharkiv Oblast, Ukraine
Combatants: Red Army; German Army
Commemorating: Liberation of Izyum
Date: August 23, 1943

Right and Opposite: *When examined like for like, the casualties sustained by the Red Army during the Belgorod–Kharkiv offensive of August 3–23, 1944, were vastly more than its opponent. Although the precise figures are impossible to ascertain, over 70,000 Soviet forces died and nearly 200,000 were wounded. The Germans lost around 10,000 killed and 20,000 wounded. However, the Russians regained Kharkhiv and would not be dislodged. The losses at Kursk and Kharkhiv meant that, for the first time since the invasion, the German Army was unable to retrive its position or the initiative.* Veselka/WikiCommons (CC BY-SA 4.0); Thechupa55/WikiCommons (CC BY-SA 4.0)

This IS-2M M1943 with an upgraded M1944 turret sits in Izyum, 125km from Ukraine's second largest city of Kharkiv (then called Kharkov). The fighting in this area raged for three years and there were four separate battles for Kharkov, as possession of the city swung back and forth from October 1941 until August 1943 when the Soviets retook it for the final time. At one point Izyum was in a Soviet salient that was pinched off and destroyed with terrible Russian losses, but the Red Army persevered, learning lessons the hard way, but learning nevertheless.

The first version of the IS-2 began production in November 1943 and kept the A-19 122mm main gun of its predecessor, but had new better quality sloped frontal armor that was more resistant yet lighter, through careful blending of its thickness from 120mm down to 60mm. There was also a new revolving commander's cupola and an additional machine-gun for AA defense. Because of the space taken by the gun and its large recoil the turret was cramped and the crew was limited to four men.

IS-2s first saw action in February 1944 in Ukraine where they performed well and were feared by the Germans, who sought to avoid frontal attacks and seek instead their weaker sides, rear, and shot trap rear turret basket. For now the better training, tactics, and battle experience of the Germans helped them maintain an edge, but it was against an unstoppable tide of Soviet production. Later in 1944 the high velocity 122mm D-25T replaced the A-19 as the main gun, with a new breech mechanism that speeded up loading. However, it was still slow to reload and still had bulky two-piece naval ammunition. After WWII the upgraded IS-2M and the IS-3 continued production of the series until 1958 and they remained in use until the 1990s with some Warsaw Pact countries.

IS-3M Heavy Tank

IS-3M

Location: Ripky,Chernihiv
Oblast, Ukraine
Combatants: Red Army;
German Army
Commemorating: The
liberation of Ripky
Date: September 26, 1943

Right and Opposite: *The
IS-3M was supplied to all
key Soviet allies with further
improvements and upgrades,
mainly to its problem-prone
powerpack.*

Opposite, Inset: *The plaque
identifies the memorial to the
liberator troops of the 58th
Tank Separate Brigade.*
Photos: Anastasiya/WikiCommons

The First Ukrainian Front attacked towards Kiev in the summer of 1943 and took back considerable amounts of territory from the invaders. The so-called battle of the Dnieper involved nearly four million Soviet troops obver 870 miles of fronts. Ripky was one of a number of locations in the Ukraine that were liberated by this drive which culminated in the battle for Kiev which was taken by November 13. The Germans counterattacked but were unable to wrest the city from Russian hands.

The IS-3 was an upgrade to the IS series that appeared in May 1945, just too late to see action in the European theater, although they took part in the September 7 Berlin victory parade where they impressed and worried Western observers. The IS-3 had a new hull design with thicker armor and a heavily sloped glacis plate, surmounted by a new more rounded, bowl-shaped turret, also with thicker armor. This sleek ergonomic design gave the IS-3 a low silhouette and a distinctive appearance that would become a trademark of all Soviet Cold War tanks.

It mounted the long-barrelled 122mm D-25T model 1943 main gun with a semiautomatic breech and was fitted with a two-chambered muzzle brake but it carried only 28 rounds of ammunition and had a slow rate of fire. Secondary armament included a 12.7mm AAMG and one or two 7.62mm MGs. The IS-3 weighed almost 46 tons, with a crew of four. It was powered by a V-2-1S V12 diesel engine that gave it a top speed of 25mph and a range of 115 miles. Production continued until mid-1946 by which time some 2,300 had been built. It served with the Red Army throughout the 1940s and 1950s.

T-34/85 Medium Tank

T-34/85

Location: Peremohy Avenue, 52/2, Kyiv, Ukraine
Combatants: Red Army; German Army
Commemorating: Liberation of Kiev
Date: November 5, 1943

This T-34/85 tank on Peremohy Avenue in Kyiv commemorates the liberation of the city on November 5, 1943, by the 3rd Guards Tank Army of the First Ukrainian Front. It was part of the wider Soviet Dneiper offensive as the Russians brought up fresh reserves, defeated a counter-attack by XLVIIIth Panzer Corps and slowly pushed the Germans back. Even though they failed to cut the rail link between the two German armies of Group Center and Group South they punched through the fortified Dneiper line and retook Kiev. Again the battle stats for the campaign are astonishing: almost four months long, involving four million men, 4,500 tanks and assault guns, 60,000 artillery pieces, and almost 5,000 aircraft fighting across a front 870 mileslong, with more than half a million men killed and over 1.5 million wounded.

The T-34/85 was produced following battle assessment of the T-34/76 and the appearance of heavier German armor such as the Panthers and Tigers at the battle of Kursk. It was decided to up-gun the existing model and three guns were put forward, though all required a new turret in order to fit. This larger three-man turret (with fitted radio) was made from an adapted prototype of the cancelled T-43's turret design. The D-5 was the original gun of choice and equipped the first production series. Then the S-18 and the ZiS-53 guns were put forward and in the end a modified ZiS-53, the ZiS-S-53, was chosen. By December 15, 1943, with the design decided on (everything else was kept virtually unchanged to ensure a smooth transition) the T-34/85 entered mass-production in early 1944 and about 11,800 were produced in that year alone.

Opposite and Left: *On November 3, 1968, this T-34/85 was installed on a concrete strip with the inscription "In memory of the Soviet tank soldiers who liberated Kiev." It commemorated the 25th anniversary of the liberation of Kyiv.* Ferran Cornellà/ WikiCommons (CC BY-SA 3.0); Prymasal/WikiCommons (CC BY-SA 4.0)

Sturmgeschütz III Ausf G Assault Gun

In 1943 the Germans supplied their allies, the Finns, with 30 Sturmgeschütz III Ausf Gs—they nicknamed them "Sturmis"—which performed very well against Russian forces. Indeed, with its long-barrelled 75mm StuK 40 L/48 main gun, it knocked out nearly 90 Soviet tanks with only 8 casualties of its own. Later, a further 29 StuG IIIs were delivered.

The German-Finnish alliance was always tenuous: the Finns needed help against the USSR but didn't want to be involved in attacks on Murmansk and Leningrad. In the end, however, after the Russians attacked in summer 1944, the Finnish armor helped to contain the assault—albeit after considerable territorial losses—and the resulting peace negotiations led to a withdrawal of German troops from Finland by September 15, 1944. Inevitably there were clashes, and former adversaries Finland and the USSR found themselves fighting together against Finland's former allies.

The Ausf G was the final version of the StuG series and by far the most common, produced by both Alkett (Berlin) and MIAG (Braunschweig/Brunswick). For this version the upper superstructure was redesigned, the driver's periscope was abandoned, the exterior boxes were deleted, the back wall of the fighting compartment was straightened and the ventilation fan on top of the superstructure relocated to the back. The loader's hatch now opened to the side, a non-rotating periscope-ring was fitted on the commander's cupola and the whole vehicle was often painted in Zimmerit anti-mine paste. All this increased height and weight.

From November 1943, Ausf Gs were fitted with the *Saukopf* (pig's head) main gun mantlet, firstly without a coaxial MG34 mount but then with one after June 1944. The Saukopf proved more effective at deflecting shots than the box-shaped original.

After WWII Finland used its StuG III tank destroyers until the 1960s, often dug-in as fixed weapons defenses.

STURMGESCHÜTZ III AUSF G

Location: Finnish Tank Museum, Parola, Finland
Commemorating: WWII
Combatants: Finnish Army; Soviet Army
Date: 1943–1944

Opposite: *Finnish StuG III Ps 531-5 "Tienhaara." The Finnish Defence Forces*

Far Left: *Note the differences between Ps 531-57 and "Marjatta" (**Left**). Ps 531-57 is a later version with the Saukopf mantlet.*

Left: *StuG III Ausf G "Marjatta," one of the Finns' most celebrated tanks. Ps 531-19, commanded by Lt M. Sartio, was responsible for seven kills in battle, including six T-34s. Two gunners made up that tally: Korpraali Olof Lagus (four) and Korpraali Reino Anttila (two and one other AFV). Note the Hakaristi (Finnish swastika) markings. This had been adopted in 1918 before WWII. Both: Balcer/ WikiCommons (CC BY 2.5)*

KV-1 (ZiS-5) Heavy Tank

This Soviet KV-1 memorial is in Ropsha, a small town set on a commanding hill 35 miles from Leningrad. From here the Germans bombarded the city. The memorial commemorates a group of tanks belonging to the 31st Guards Heavy Tank Regiment of the Leningrad Front which broke through the enemy lines here on January 19, 1944, and destroyed a large German artillery position.

It's an original tank with visible battle damage, knocked out by a German anti-tank gun during the fighting. The Germans were as disconcerted when they met the KV-1 as they were when they first saw the T-34, its heavy armor proved impervious to anything but their 88mm. It was armed with a 76mm M1941 ZiS-5 main gun—a modified version of that used in the T-34/76 and it used the same Trashutin V-2 V12 diesel engine.

The main differences between the two tanks were the KV-1's heavier armor, which made it slower, and its roomier turret, which made firing easier. However, it was also more expensive to make. The KVs were designed for infantry support rather than the T-34's tank-fighting role. It was produced from 1939 until 1943. In 1940 it was given a new mantlet and mounted the F-32 76mm main gun. Another version—the KV-1E—appeared the same year with additional bolted-on appliqué armor. In 1941 it was uparmored with 25–35mm added to the turret, hull front, and sides, with the turret now cast instead of welded and armed with the longer-barrelled ZiS-5—this tank's gun. 1942's version was given a fully cast turret and again uparmored, and used an improved engine. 1943's lighter KV-1S was made faster with thinner armor and a smaller, lower turret housing the 85 mm D-5T gun. The series was then discontinued, giving way to the IS and SU heavy tanks.

KV-1 (ZIS-5)

Location: Ropsha, Leningrad oblast, Russia
Combatants: Red Army; German Army
Commemorating: The breakthrough on the Leningrad Front
Date: January 19, 1944

Opposite and Left: *The plaque reads, "the point where, on January 19, 1944, tankers newly arrived from Oranienbaum and Pulkovo districts completed the ring of steel around the Fascist murderers who were bombarding Lenin's city with their artillery."* MrStepanovka/WikiCommons (CC BY 3.0)

IS-2 M1943 Heavy Tank

Location: St Petersberg
Combatants: Red Army; German Army
Commemorating: The Kirov Plant and the siege of Leningrad
Date: September 8, 1941– January 27, 1944

Right and Opposite: *The siege of Leningrad is one of the longest in history—872 days, from September 8, 1941, to January 27, 1944: as many as 1.5 million people died in Leningrad and a further 1.4 million were evacuated, many dying during the process. When one considers that the combined UK/US deaths—military and civilian—during the period totaled 870,000, it puts Leningrad's tribulations into perspective. In February 1965 poet M.A. Dudin suggested the "Green Belt of Glory," a complex of memorials around Leningrad. This IS-2 is one of these in the Kirovsky district.* Sbarichev/WikiCommons; GAlexandrova/WikiCommons (CC BY-SA 4.0)

This Russian IS-2 sits on a plinth outside the Kirov Plant in St Petersburg—Russia's second-largest city after Moscow—in memory of the critical role it played in 1941–1944 during the siege of Leningrad, as the city was then called. Beginning in 1940, it produced KV-1 and T-34 tanks. When the Germans attacked on June 22, 1941, Leningrad was one of the key objectives and so in July some 15,000 workers and their families and machinery were relocated east to Russia's Central Asian tank industrial complex, called Tankograd, at the Chelyabinsk Kirov Plant. The remaining equipment stayed operational, together with that of the Obukhov Factory on the other side of the city, during the long, harsh siege that now unfolded. Leningrad's entire civilian population was mobilized to help build anti-tank fortifications and defenses around the city's perimeter. It was then was cut off, blockaded and bombarded for the next 872 days, claiming the lives of over a million Russians, many dying of starvation during the winter. A trickle of food and fuel supplies reached the city across the southern part of Lake Ladoga by barge in the summer and by truck and ice-borne sled in winter, enough to keep the fighters going.

This was the most lethal siege in world history, with large parts of the city systematically destroyed and deliberate starvation used as a weapon. Finally, on January 14, 1944, the Leningrad–Novgorod Offensive was launched with the express purpose of relieving the city. A fortnight later German troops had been pushed 60 miles away and the Red Army had regained control of the Moscow–Leningrad rail route. On January 27 Stalin declared that the siege was lifted.

The Kirov Plant remained an important industrial complex long after the war and still exists today, although it stopped building tanks in 1991.

T-34/76 Medium Tank

Location: Liberation Memorial, Chernivtsi, Ukraine
Combatants: Red Army; German Army
Commemorating: Liberation of Chernivtsi
Date: March 25, 1944

Opposite: *The first tank to enter Chernivisti on March 25, 1944, was the vehicle of Lt Pavel Nikitin who knocked out three enemy tanks. Nikitin died on either the 25th or 26th and is remembered on this plaue and buried in the Russian cemetery. There is a Guards badge on the left-hand side of the turret.*
Both: Maupa96/Wiki Commons (CC BY-SA 3.0)

This Russian T-34/76 is part of the Liberation Memorial celebrating the relief of Chernivtsi on March 25, 1944. Although deservedly famous the T-34 was not without its faults, in design, manufacture and usage—up to 40 percent of its losses were operational rather than in combat. The early versions of 1941–1943 were often badly made with a transmission prone to break down, poor armor welds, an engine that was sensitive to dust with an air-filtration system that never worked properly, and the tracks used to regularly break apart. The original turret was cramped and could only fit two, with the commander having to seek targets and aim and fire the gun simultaneously. The sloped turret constricted space and limited the amount of ammunition capable of being carried and the electrical mechanism for rotating it was weak. Pre-1944 Soviet AP shells were of a low quality and prone to splitting apart on impact. Only 1 in 10 T-34s (company commanders) were actually equipped with a radio while every German tank had one—the rest of the Russian tank crews in each company signaled with flags. The Germans soon learned to recognize and target the command tanks. Russian tank tactics often contributed to the high losses they sustained, along with poor crew training and leadership. Over-extended spearheads were surrounded, cut off, and destroyed regularly, but tanks were encouraged to penetrate deeply without infantry support and fight for as long as they could. They were sometimes used bunched together en masse in suicidal charges—often with the deliberate intention of ramming an enemy and negating both vehicles. Despite this, as with the US Sherman, the T-34 was produced in such numbers (49,000 were made during the war) that the loss of tens of thousands in combat were more than replaced. Faults were continuously corrected, production simplified and tactics developed that ensured its survival and prosperity.

SU-100 Tank Destroyer

SU-100

Location: Partyzanska Street, Alushta, Crimea
Combatants: Red Army: German Army
Commemorating: The 45th anniversary of the liberation of Alushta
Date: April 15, 1944

Right: *This monument to the liberators of Alushta was built for the 45th anniversary of the victory.*
Дмитрий Скляренко/WikiCommons (CC BY 3.0)

Far Right: *This photo was taken through the window of the #52 Simferopol–Alushta–Yalta trolleybus.*
Cmapm/WikiCommons

Opposite: *This Su-100 is at Penza, southeast of Moscow.*
Independeht/WikiCommons (CC BY-SA 3.0)

Situated on the coast in the southern part of the Crimean peninsula, Alushta's current status is disputed between Ukraine and Russia. In a small park off Partyzanska Street in the city is an SU-100 self-propelled tank destroyer, perched on a high monument.

The SU-100—*Samokhodnaya Ustanovka (self-propelled carriage)*—was the peak of Soviet tank destroyer development in WWII. With a low profile and thick sloping frontal armor, its main gun was the powerful 100mm Gorlitskiy D-10 (based on a pre-WWII naval gun) and it carried 33 rounds of ammunition: 18 x AP and 15 x HE/FRAG. With AP the D-10 could penetrate any part of a German Panther from over a mile away. However, its barrel was very long with an overhang of 10ft and it had limited traverse and elevation, requiring the crew to aim the whole vehicle in the direction

it needed to fire. It had a crew of four, with the driver sitting at front left and the gun to his immediate right. To the right side of the hull superstructure there was a raised cupola with vision ports in the roof for the commander; a loader's hatch was set to the left of it.

Powered by a Kirimov V-2-34M 12-cylinder diesel engine giving it a top speed of 30mph and a range of 200 miles, SU-100s were often seen with two or four extra external tubular fuel tanks attached to each side of the hull rear, for the upper superstructure of the vehicle only extended to the midway point. It was used extensively in the final year of WWII, feared by the Germans and popular with its crews. Some 2,300 were built and remained in Soviet service up until the 1950s, but well beyond by other allied nations such as Cuba, Egypt, and North Korea.

ISU-152 Assault Gun

Right: *Front view of a ISU-152 in the "35 years—Victory Park" at Kineshma, Ivanovo oblast, Russia.*
Ferran Cornellà/WikiCommons (CC BY-SA 3.0)

Opposite: *The plaque identifies this ISU-152 as being employed by 142nd Division in the summer 1944 battles around Priozersk.*
Lvova Anastasiya/Wiki Commons

Karelia is debateable land: Finns and Swedes fought for it in the 13th century. In the 19th it was the Finns and the Soviets, the latter claiming it after the Winter War of 1939. Finland "liberated" Karelia in 1941–1944 but then had to cede it back to the Soviet Union.

This ISU-152 assault gun—now in a park near the historic Korela fortress in central Priozersk—is an original which took part in hostilities to liberate the city from the Germans in the summer of 1942. A fully enclosed 152mm gun-howitzer, the original SU-152 was built onto the KV-1S tank chassis, but when that vehicle gave way to the new IS tanks, their chassis was used instead and the SU-152 was renamed ISU-152. Production started at the Chelyabinsk factory in December 1943. The ISU-152 was armed with the 152.4mm ML-20S model 1937 howitzer, with a barrel length of over 13ft 9.5in (27.9 calibres) and a maximum range of 6,780yd. It carried only 21 rounds of two-piece (shell and charge) AP and HE ammunition. Its AP round weighed 48.78 kg and it had a rate of fire of two/three rounds/minute; however, the small amount of ammunition carried necessitated rapid and regular replenishment. Later ISU-152 versions had a newer longer-barrelled gun, up to over 16ft (32.3 calibres), with a maximum range of 14,200ft. It was manned by a crew of five. Since the ISU-152 had no turret, aiming the gun was time consuming, requiring the repositioning of the entire vehicle using only the tracks. This made its use primarily one of mobile artillery to support infantry and armor attacks and city assaults. As a heavy assault gun the ISU-152 was an extremely valuable weapon in urban combat operations. Its excellent armor gave it good protection from most German anti-tank guns, allowing it to get close and blast the most

heavily fortified and reinforced enemy strongpoints. It continued in production until 1959 and in service into the 1970s receiving other upgrades and was used by several countries including China, North Korea, Egypt, Poland and Romania.

PzKpfw IV Ausf J and T-34/85 Medium Tanks

PZKPFW IV AUSF J AND T-34/85

Location: Battle of Dukla Pass Monument, outside Svidník, Slovakia
Commemorating: Battle of Dukla Pass
Combatants: German Army; Soviet Army and Czechoslovak Corps
Date: September 8–October 28, 1944

This monument of a Russian T-34/85 riding over a German Panzer IV Ausf J is in the Carpathian Mountains on the Polish-Slovak border. The battle that was fought at Dukla was one of most bitter contests on the Eastern Front, as the Russian Army with an attached Czechoslovak Corps attempted to dislodge the German and Hungarian forces from their fortified mountain strongholds. It took considerably longer than the five days expected and cost the attackers over 130,000 men, while the Axis forces lost 30,000. Even after the pass was forced the battle continued in eastern Slovakia as Soviet forces tried to outflank the Germans, who by this time had crushed the Slovak national uprising the Russians were trying to support.

The PzKpfw IV was the most produced German tank of the war after the PzKpfw III, with some 8,500 of all versions built. Variants included the Sturmgeschütz IV assault gun and the Jagdpanzer IV tank destroyer, the Wirbelwind (whirlwind)

self-propelled quad-2cm flak gun, and the Sturmpanzer, nicknamed Brummbär (grouch), a self-propelled heavy assault gun armed with a 15cm Sturmhaubitze 43 L/12.

Robust and reliable, the PzKpfw IV saw service in all combat theaters and received continuous upgrades and design modifications—chiefly increases in armor thickness and the size of its main gun which had the negative effect of reducing speed considerably. The Ausf J was the final model of the series, produced June 1944–March 1945 when the German response to the T-34—the PzKpfw V Panther—replaced it, although PzKpfw IVs continued to be manufactured by Nibelungenwerke in Austria until the end of the war.

The Ausf J was powered by a Maybach HL120TRM engine delivering a top speed of 24mph and had a range of 320km. It was armed with a 7.5cm KwK40 L/48 main gun and two 7.92mm MG13s, but it sacrificed important items (such as powered turret traverse) or econmies of production.

Right: *Mapboard showing the battle: the Russians are in red, the Germans in blue. Note Svidnik at bottom*

Far Right: *Just outside Svidnik stands the famous memorial used on our back cover and here.*

Opposite: *One of the many T-34/85s left in situ on the Dukla Pass battlefield.*
Photos: Tom Timmermans

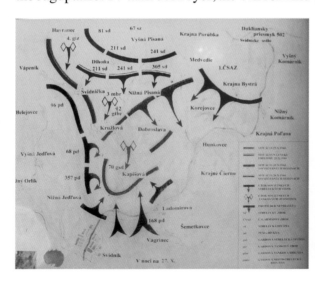

PzKpfw III Ausf H Medium Tank

PZKPFW III AUSF H

Location: Povitroflots'kyi Avenue 28, Kyiv
Commemorating: WWII in Ukraine
Combatants: German Army; Soviet Army
Date: 1944

This PzKpfw III Ausf H sits outside the Academy of the Armed Forces of the Ukraine in Kyiv (Kiev). It is an original from 1944 that was blown off a pontoon bridge into the River Bug during a Soviet bombing raid. It was recovered and renovated in the 1990s.

The PzKpfw III ended up as the German medium infantry support tank, but when designed in the early 1930s it was supposed to be the main battle tank of the German Army in the 1940s. Combat experience soon showed that it was underarmored and undergunned against heavier Allied (French Char B-1 Bis and the British Matilda) and Russian (T-34 and KV) tanks.

However, designed with a turret ring that was capable of upgunning, later models changed the initial 37mm "popgun" and were armed with a larger 50mm gun; they were also uparmored. Thus the PzKpfw III series was able to continue in service. It performed well, but by 1942—even after upgunning again to the early PzKpfw IV's short-barreled gun 75mm—it had been superseded by the more powerful PzKpfw IV. Nevertheless, because of its reliability and prevalence, the PzKpfw III still had a role to play on the battlefield—as command and communications vehicles, infantry support, and by using its proven chassis to produce the Sturmgeschütz III.

About 300 of the Ausf H version were produced from October 1940 until April 1941. They were fitted with extra 30mm armor plates on the hull front and rear and the superstructure front, increasing the weight of the tank. To compensate for this the Ausf H was given 40cm wide tracks, redesigned wheels, stronger torsion bars, and a new transmission. It was powered by a 12-cylinder Maybach HL 108 TR engine, giving a top speed of 22mph and a range of 103 miles. It was armed with a 5cm KwK L/42 main gun plus two 7.92mm MG 34s—one coaxial with the main gun in the turret and one in the hull front. It was used in the Balkans, Russia, and North Africa.

The PzKpfw III in Kyiv. Unlike the T-34, the PzKpfw III had a three-man turret which allowed the commander to concentrate on commanding. It meant that superior tactics kept the crew alive longer, and experienced tank crew compensated for the tank's shortcomings.
Photos: Pavlo1/WikiCommons (CC BY-SA 4.0)

IS-2 Heavy Tank

Location: Muzeum Czynu Zbrojnego, Krakow, Poland
Commemorating: Soviet forces of WWII
Combatants: Red Army; German Army
Date: 1944–1945

Right: *This IS-2 was knocked out near Summa, on the Karelian Isthmus, during what the Finns called the Continuation War, the hostilities between the German and Finnish armies and the Soviets that started some 15 months after the Winter War.* Finnish Army photographer/ WikiCommons

Opposite: *The IS-2 outside the Krakow museum.* Zygmunt Put Zetpe0202/WikiCommons

This Russian IS-2 has been sitting in front of the military Muzeum Czynu Zbrojnego in Krakow for over 40 years. It is an original Soviet tank that served in the war all the way to Berlin and was given to the museum by the Polish Army on January 26, 1969, and restored in 2006–2007.

The IS series was developed to succeed the KV heavy tank on which it was based, with thicker armor and a heavier main gun to counter the Tigers and Panthers, but also to be used as a breakthrough tank firing HE munitions against entrenchments, anti-tank guns, and bunkers. Based on a modified KV chassis, it kept the KV suspension together with the standard Model V-2 12-cylinder diesel engine, but by lowering the driving sprockets, idlers, and return rollers and modifying the hull roof, space was made for a larger turret ring.

The original IS-1 had an 85mm main gun, whereas the IS-2 mounted a massive 122mm A19 main gun fitted with a double-baffle muzzle-brake. The two-part shells were so large only 22 could be carried at a time. It was also armed with three 7.62mm Degtyarev machine guns—one coaxial with the main gun and two in ball mounts, one in the hull front and the other in the rear of the turret. The IS-2 entered service in April 1944 and 2,250 were produced by the end of the year. Combat experience led to the next version, the IS-3, which had thicker front armor of 200mm compared to IS-2's 120mm and a new streamlined cast turret, however it did not see action before the war ended. IS-2s and IS-3s remained in Red Army use until the 1990s and later still by Cuba, China, and North Korea.

T-34/85 Medium Tank

T-34/85

Location: Liberation Memorial, Jasnogórska, Gliwice, Poland
Combatants: Red Army; German Army
Commemorating: General Jozef Kimbar and the Polish I Armoured Corps
Date: 1944–45

This Russian T-34/85 at the Liberation Memorial, Jasnogórska in Gliwice is a Red Army original that was part of the force which liberated the city in 1945. Gliwice is a border city in Silesia, south Poland—called Gliwice in Polish, Gleiwitz in German, and Hlivice in Czech—and was a place of mixed cultures. It was at Gliwice that the Germans created a pretext for the invasion of Poland and they also built a concentration camp there, a subcamp of the infamous Auschwitz.

On January 24, 1945, it was occupied by the Red Army, most of the German population was expelled, and the city was placed under Polish administration agreed at the 1945 Potsdam Conference. The memorial commemorates the Polish I Armoured Corps—an armored formation of the Polish People's Army 1944–1945 commanded by General Józef Kimbar (who transferred from the Red Army)—which saw combat in Germany before being dispersed to garrisons in Poland and deactivated on October 5, 1945.

The T-34/85 was an upgunning response to the German 88mm-armed PzKpfw V Panther and PzKpfw VI Tiger which were appearing on the battlefield by 1943 and against which the T-34/76 struggled. Prototypes were built with new 85mm guns mounted in the original M1942 turret, but it was found too small to fit and so a new T-34-85 turret was designed. Reconfigured for a three-man crew of gunner, loader, and commander, with full vision capability and full radio equipment, it was now armed first with the 85mm D-5 (a converted 85mm 52-K anti-aircraft gun) and then with the similar 85mm ZiS-53 or ZiS-S-53 gun, both of which were simpler, easier to operate, and gave a higher rate of fire.

The T-34/85 continued to be produced postwar and was modernized in 1960 and 1969 with new engines and external components.

Opposite and Left: *Józef Kimbar was a Russian general sent to command the the Armored and Motorized Brigade of the First Polish Army in May 1944. He took over command of I Armored Corps on September 8 and was promoted major general on August 9, 1945. During his tenure of office, Polish I Armored Corps fought northeast of Dresden, then as part of the forces around Berlin, ending up around Prague. During this time the unit knocked out 178 AFVs and took 3,900 prisoners, losing 444 killed, 980 wounded, and 143 AFVs in the process.*
Both: Radosław Drożdżewski (User:Zwiadowca21)/ WikiCommons (CC BY-SA 4.0)

Location: Hrib Svobode (Liberty Hill), Ilirska Bistrica, Slovenia
Combatants: Yugoslav Army; Slovene Partisans; German Army
Commemorating: Yugoslav Army; Slovene Partisans
Date: WWII

Right: *Originally supplied to the Yugoslavs, M4A3 Sherman outside the Park of Military History, Pivka, Slovenia.* canvas 123/WikiCommons (CC0)

Opposite: *The United States and Britain supplied significant amounts of materiel to the Soviet Union and did not expect to get paid for it. Britain alone supplied 7,000+ aircraft, 5,200 tanks, antitank guns, trucks, aircraft engines, etc. The United States supplied $11,000 million worth of materiel. Other countries, too, received aid. Yugoslavia, for example, received $32 million worth of aid, including M3A3 Stuarts, as here.*

M3A3 Stuart Light Tank

Liberty Hill (also called Brinšek's Hill) is a park in the center of the town of Ilirska Bistrica, in Slovenia with three monuments. At the top is a strikingly large white cube with holes and pillars under which is a tomb where soldiers of the Fourth Yugoslav Army and other local fighters are buried. It is also a memorial of Serbia's largest concentration camp, which claimed the lives of an estimated 80,000–100,000 people.

Further down is is a monument dedicated to the TIGR (Revolutionary Organization of the Julian March: Trieste-Istria-Gorizia-Rijeka), Slovene anti-fascist partisan fighters active between 1927 and 1941. The third monument on the hill is an artillery gun and an American M3A3 Stuart light tank, both of which took part in the liberation of Ilirska Bistrica in World War II. It is painted with the flag of the Kingdom of Yugoslavia (1929–1946), but also has a star on the hull front, indicating the Federal People's Republic of Yugoslavia (1946–1963).

Although already outdated and unwanted by the US military, M3A1s and M3A3s were delivered to Yugoslavia and the Far East during 1944. The M3A3, produced in 1942 until October 1943, was the last in the series. It had a new sloped and thickened welded hull, a longer turret, and a more sloped armored superstructure, along with new periscopes for the driver and commander and a different position for the driver's hatch. It was armed with M6 gun and three M1919A4 machine guns. Both M3A1s and M3A3s were used by the Yugoslav First Tank Brigade, especially in the liberation of Mostar, Knin, and Trieste. M3A3s were also supplied to the Soviets who thought very little of them, criticizing their weak armor and weaponry, and too narrow tracks.

T-34/85 Medium Tank

Sitting outside the prison complex it helped liberate in Brandenburg an der Havel, Germany, this Russian T-34/85. From August 1940 to April 1945, 2,380 inmates were killed here by the Nazis, who used it to jail "dangerous elements"—criminals, political prisoners, draft resisters, and POWs. As a designated execution center it was supplied with and used a Tegel Fallbeil, a guillotine made by the inmates of another prison in Berlin.

The T-34/85 was the upgrade of the T-34/76 and first saw action in elite Red Guards battalions at the beginning of 1944 to instant acclaim from their crews. By the end of the year it outnumbered older versions and formed the bulk of the tanks for the huge Operation Bagration, the offensive to take Berlin. Its high silhouette and broad turret were a disadvantage especially when attacked from the side, but the high-velocity and range of its 85mm gave it a powerful punch. In the urban warfare that ensued a new threat emerged in the form of the Panzerfaust, a one-man, single-use, pre-loaded launch tube that fired a high explosive anti-tank (HEAT) warhead, that created massive internal spalling, killing the crew and destroying equipment. To try and cope with this crews took to improvising outer layers of protection on top of the tank's armor, even using welded bed frames. In the battles on the eastern frontier T-34/85s made short work of the old-fashioned light tanks used by the Japanese. It continued to be produced after the war up until 1958 and saw use in over 50 countries. In the end over 80,000 were made, making it the second most produced tank in the world after the T-54/55.

T-34/85

Location: Anton-Saefkow-Allee 17, Brandenburg an der Havel, Germany
Combatants: Red Army; German Army
Commemorating: The liberation of the New Brandenburg Prison
Date: April 27, 1945

Opposite and Above Left: *"Thanks to the Soviet soldiers of the 32nd Guards Armored and 62nd Guards Cavalry Regiments for freeing the antifascist fighters from the one-time fascist Brandenburg jail.* Wald1siedel/ WikiCommons (CC BY-SA 4.0); Judith Richmann/ WikiCommons (CC BY-SA 4.0)

Below Left: *Memorial to the men of many nations who were executed here.* Wald1siedel/ WikiCommons (CC BY-SA 4.0)

T-34/76 M1943 Medium Tank

In the Tiergarten on Straße des 17 Juni in Berlin, sit two Soviet T-34 tanks flanking the Soviet War Memorial that commemorates the 90,000–100,000 Soviet soldiers who died during the battle for the German capital from April 16 to May 2, 1945, and the actual grave of some 2,000. The statistics of the battle are commensurate with others on the Eastern Front—some 3,500,000 men all told, with 7,000 tanks and AFVs, 50,000 artillery pieces and 9,000 aircraft met in the final uncompromising clash. For the Germans it was their last stand, that would result in the destruction of the city, the death of Hitler, the unconditional surrender of the Berlin garrison, and a week later the capitulation of all German Forces. A single eastern defensive line—German Ninth Army and Fourth Panzer Army—based on the Seelow Heights (known as the "Gates of Berlin") held for a week before being broken and encircled. This meant that they could not retreat the 55 miles to Berlin to help with its defense, and the battle there became bitter block-to-block urban warfare between the Red Army and a range of small units.

The surrounded German forces—up to 150,000 men—fought to break out of the encirclement: the battle of Halbe. In the end some 25–30,000 managed to do so at the third attempt, and joined Twelfth Army, who had been attacking towards them. These forces moved west in order to surrender to the US Army. They left behind over 30,000 dead and thousands captured.

The T-34/76 M1943 version was the same as the previous M1942 except for the addition of a commander's cupola. It was armed with the high velocity 76.2mm F-34 main gun in a hexagonal turret, however because there were several manufacturers of the turrets across the USSR there was quite a bit of variation.

T-34/76 M1943

Location: Straße des 17. Juni, Tiergarten, Berlin
Combatants: Red Army; German Army
Commemorating: Russian war dead of the Battle of Berlin
Date: April 16–May 2, 1945

Opposite and Below:
T-34/76 M1943 in Berlin. Over the period December 1943 to April 1944 the T-34/76 M1942/3 model was replaced by the T-34/85 at the three main T-34 production plants. Mike Peel (www.mikepeel.net); Klearchos Kapoutsis/WikiCommons (CC BY 2.0)

Chapter 8: Outside Europe

The M3 medium tank was named the Lee in British service; those with a modified British turret, the Grant. Quickly replaced by the M4 Sherman, M3s were used against the Japanese in India where there are a number of preserved examples. This photograph is of an M3 in June 1942 at Fort Knox. LoC

Outside the European theaters of WWII, armor played roles of varying importance. In the deserts of North Africa, where the tide of battle ebbed and flowed according to the stretch of critical supply lines, movement was pre-eminent and armor (and mobile artillery) absolutely critical to the outcome all events.

For almost three years (June 10, 1940–May 13, 1943) the advantage oscillated between the principal antagonists: the German Afrika Korps, with Italian assistance, and the British and Commonwealth Eighth Army. Finally, after the Royal Navy and Desert Air Force had curtailed German resupply from Europe while succeeding in building up much larger British forces, the tide was turned at the second battle of El Alamein and with the subsequent Operation Torch Landings of November 8–16, 1942, opening another front in the Germans' rear, the campaign was ended in the first Allied victory of the war.

Against the Japanese in the Pacific, the USMC used tanks to fight infantry, mainly because the Japanese never really produced a tank capable of adequately fighting the M4, tending to use theirs as assault guns. The Sherman first fought with the Marines at the battle of Tarawa (November 20–23, 1943) and was easily the most powerful tank in the Pacific making short work of any Japanese armor. The USMC also used the Sherman M4A3R3, as well as light and medium tanks, all mounting flamethrowers, as close assault weapons.

The Russians with BTs and T-26s, ultimately outperformed the Japanese Type 89 I-Go and Type 97 Chi-ha medium tanks at the battles of Khalkhyn Gol (May 11–September 15, 1939). Later on August 9–September 2, 1945, their T-34 tanks, forged in the furnace of the Eastern Front, made short work of the Japanese Kwantung Army in Manchuria.

The Japanese did build later tanks and SPs such as the 75mm Type 3 Chi-Nu and 75mm Type 1 No-Hi I tank destroyer, but only in very limited numbers.

Opposite: *M3 medium lit up for Christmas! This is in Juiz de Fora, Brazil.* Leandro Neumann Ciuffo/ WikiCommons (CC BY 2.0)

Below: *A panorama of tanks at the Indian Cavalry Tank Museum, Maharashtra.* Mohit S/WikiCommons (CC BY 2.0)

M4A1 Sherman II Medium Tank

M4A1 SHERMAN II

Location: Alexandria-Marsa Matrouh Rd, Markaz El Alamein, Egypt
Combatants: British Army; Italian and German Army
Commemorating: The second battle of El Alamein
Date: October 23– November 11, 1942

Outside (and inside) the superb Military Museum on the Alexandria-Marsa Matrouh road in El Alamein is a wonderful selection of AFVs and artillery used by both sides during the Desert War of 1940–1943, including a British M4A1 or Sherman II. This model was the first of its kind to go into battle in WWII, seeing action in the critical second battle of El Alamein when the Allies defeated the Germans and turned the tide in the North African theater. They had been rushed to the British after the fall of Tobruk and, having been hastily modified to British specifications, were named Sherman II. They were formed into heavy squadrons to beef up other units possessing Stuarts and Crusaders.

Armor played a vital role in the battle. Over 1,000 Allied tanks fought against 550 of the Axis and the Shermans with their 75mm, along with the Grants, gave Montgomery's tank force a powerful new punch. Although they would suffer later when up against German Tigers and Panthers, these two tanks could engage their enemy counterparts at the same range and use their HE to good effect against anti-tank guns and infantry. As more Shermans arrived, including the successor of the Sherman II, the M4A2 or Sherman III, more British units converted to them.

The British were surprised by the speed of the German retreat from El Alamein and failed to follow up their success, allowing the Germans—masters of orderly fighting withdrawals—to conduct a text-book retreat. However Montgomery's caution reflected the care he took with his troops and his knowledge of the forthcoming Torch Landings of November 8–16, 1942, which would bring US troops into action and meant the Germans were fatally fighting on two fronts. By the end of WWII the British received far more M4 Shermans than any other ally, approximately 17,000 in total.

Right: *Italian Semovente da 75/18 at the El Alamein Museum.*

Opposite: *Lend-Lease kicked in to help British forces rebuild their strength—something Rommel's Afrika Korps couldn't do. At left, an M4A2; at right an unusual sight: an M3 turret on a Universal Carrier.*
Both: Heather Cowper from Bristol, UK (CC BY 2.0)

T-34/85 Medium Tank

The magnificent Zaisan Memorial is on a hill in the southern part of the city of Ulaanbaatar, the capital of Mongolia. It commemorates in a giant illustrated ring at the top of the hill the allied Mongolian and Soviet troops who died in service either against the Japanese or the Germans in WWII, as well as showing other scenes of Mongolian-Soviet cooperation. In 2003 a T-34 tank that had previously been located elsewhere in the city was brought to bottom of the hill and mounted on a tall plinth, on whose side is a schematic of the route fought from Moscow to Berlin.

At the time of WWII Mongolia was ruled by an indigenous communist government that was in close alliance with the USSR and its geographical position made it a buffer between Japan and the Soviet Union. The Soviets had begun to help Mongolia form a modern army since the 1920s but the high rate of illiteracy and lack of military infrastructure made it a slow process. On the eve of WWII Mongolia provided the Russians with volunteers and raw materials but they also subsidized various Soviet units, including the Revolutionary Mongolia Tank Brigade and other armored squadrons.

Mongolian troops took part in the 1939 battle of Khalkin Gol that took place May 11–September 15, 1939, during which the Japanese Kwantung Army launched a large bombing raid deep inside Mongolian territory and attacked across the border in divisional strength. Mongolia also took part in the Soviet August 9–20, 1945, invasion of Manchuria as part of the Soviet-Mongolian Cavalry Mechanized Group, providing several cavalry divisions, the 7th Motorized Armored Brigade, the Armored Car Brigade and the 3rd Artillery Regiment. Postwar it continued to buy Soviet hardware with which to equip its own armed forces.

Opposite: *The T-34/85 at the Zaisan Memorial remembers the Mongolian Brigade who fought from Moscow in 1943 through to Berlin.* alex_and_stacy/WikiCommons (CC BY 2.0)

Left and Below Left: *The Zaisan Memorial. Included on the inside face are scenes that show the amity between Mongolia and the USSR, including the defeat of the Japanese at Khalhkin Gol in 1939 and victory over Hitler's Germany.* Francisco Anzola/WikiCommons (CC BY 2.0); Gyula Péta/WikiCommons (CC BY 3.0)

M4A2(75) SHERMAN

Location: Garapan Beach, Saipan
Combatants: Imperial Japanese Army; US Army
Commemorating: Battle of Saipan
Date: June 15–July 9, 1944

Right: *This wreck is off Tarawa, Kiribati. The bloody assault on Tarawa in November 1943 taught the US forces many important lessons about amphibious warfare, but the cost was enormous.* Roisterer/WikiCommons (CC BY-SA 3.0).

Opposite: *One of three M4A2(75) Shermans off Oleai and Susupe beaches, Saipan. There was a surprising amount of tank action on Saipan considering the terrain. The Japanese 9th Tank Regiment had 90 tanks, two companies of which were on Guam. They attacked the beachhead but were seen off by the M4A2s of 2nd Tank Battalion. On Guam—a larger island than Saipan—there was also tank combat.* RaksyBH/Shutterstock

M4A2(75) Sherman Medium Tank

At the same time as the D-Day landings took place on the Europe's western shoreline a US fleet embarked from Pearl Harbor in Hawaii to begin the American invasion of Saipan. A strategically important island in the Mariana Archipelago less than 15 miles long and 5 miles wide, it consists of a central chain of mountains with a narrow coastal strip. Taking Saipan would put Tokyo within range of US bombers.

Following a huge naval bombardment from a massive US fleet of over 500 ships, between June 15 and July 9, 1944, an uncompromising battle (the fiercest of the three major battles in the Marianas) was fought against fanatical Japanese troops who refused to surrender. On June 15 thousands of US Marines landed along with 13 Shermans of the 3rd, 4th and 5th Tank Battalions, including four with E4-5 flamethrowers replacing the 75mm main gun. Littering the seabed around the island in clear shallow water lie aircraft, amphibious vehicles,

ships, and tanks from the battle. Visible just offshore of the invasion beaches on the southwest side of the island are three half submerged M4s which never made it—one pierced by an anti-tank round, the others lost when they sank in a deep water hole while negotiating the reef. Despite heavy resistance and over 2,000 casualties, 8,000 Marines managed to reach the shore on the first morning and by the end of the day some 20,000 troops had established a beachhead.

The battle then moved inland and into the mountains, where the Japanese had also prepared extensive defenses based around the 1,550ft Mount Tapotchau—the island's highest point. Savage and bloody, waged with no quarter asked nor given, at the end of the battle the Americans had lost 3,426 killed and 10,364 wounded; the Japanese lost a staggering 29,000 men and a further 22,000 civilians were killed, many of whom were suicides.

Type 97 Chi-Ha Medium Tank

TYPE 97 CHI-HA

Location: Beach Road Pathway, Garapan, Saipan
Combatants: Imperial Japanese Army; US Army
Commemorating: Battle of Saipan
Date: June 15–July 9, 1944

This destroyed Imperial Japanese Army Type 97 Chi-Ha medium tank sits on the roof of a bunker between Susupi and Garapan on the west coast of the island of Saipan. There were many more Japanese soldiers on Saipan than the Americans realized—some 30,000—hidden in bunkers and casemates, spider holes and tunnels. They also had armor resources, although defensive tactics dictated that for the most part they were hull down and dug in, sometimes right up to their turrets.

The Type 97 Chi-Ha was the most-produced Japanese medium tank of WWII, some 2,000 made 1938–1943. It had a low silhouette and was of a riveted rather than welded construction with a four-man crew of driver, bow machine-gunner, and two turret crew. It was designed for supporting infantry and carried a short-barrelled Type 97 57mm main gun that had a low muzzle velocity and no elevation: the gunner had to use his shoulder! The Chi-Ha also carried twoType 97 7.7mm machine guns, one on the front left of the hull and the other in a ball mount on the rear of the turret. The turret had full traverse and a commander's cupola, with the thickest armor (25mm) on the gun mantlet. It was powered by a Mitsubishi V12 SA12200VD air-cooled diesel engine giving it a top speed of 38 kmh (24 mph) and a range of 210km (130 miles).

During the Battle of Saipan, 44 Type 97s of the IJA's 9th Tank Regiment, along with other Japanese units' Type 95 tanks, combined in a final desperate all-out counter-attack against the American beachhead in what was one of the largest tank engagements of the Pacific theater.

They were outperformed and easily knocked out by the heavier American Shermans, M3 75mm half-tracks, 37mm anti-tank guns, and bazookas.

Opposite and Above Left:
Two views of the wreck of a Type 97 on Beach Road, Saipan, amongst the flame trees (Delonix regia). There are a number of other Type 97 wrecks on the island. Peter Rood/WikiCommons (CC BY-SA 2.0); Abasaa/ WikiCommons (CC BY-SA 2.0)

Below Left: *And this is what it should look like! The ShinHoTo (new turret) Chi-Ha had a 47mm main armament, a turret crew of three, and entered combat at the battle of Corregidor in 1942. This one came from Shumshu Island in near Sakhalin and today can be seen in Moscow's Victory Park.* Alan Wilson/WikiCommons (CC BY-SA 2.0)

M4A3(75)W Sherman Medium Tank

M4A3(75)W SHERMAN

Location: Iwo Jima
Commemorating: Battle of Iwo Jima
Combatants: Imperial Japanese Army; US Army
Date: February 19–March 26, 1945

Right: *Heavier than the M4A2, the USMC M4A3s had to be delivered to the bach in landing ships, medium, rather than landing craft. Two of the tank battalions had M4A3s (including one tank in each troop with a flamethrower) and the third M4A2s. This photograph shows a USMC flamethrowing M4A3R3 in action. A 1945 report on armor on Iwo Jima said of the flamethrowers, "This weapon gave excellent results when it worked and could reach the target ... [although] mechanical trouble and poor fuel reduced the efficiency approximately 75% ... [and] it failed to function at all 25% of the time." USMC via WikiCommons*

There are many wrecked tanks, guns and vehicles dotted about the island of Iwo Jima, site of another ferocious battle between the US and Japan in WWII. This destroyed and rusting Sherman M4A3 is in the center of the island, near the western end of the airport runway. It belonged to the USMC's 4th Tank Battalion and was knocked out during the battle that witnessed some of the fiercest and bloodiest fighting of the Pacific war.

Although the outcome was never really in doubt as over 100,000 Americans with 500 ships fought 21,000 Japanese, the tenacity of the IJA ensured they paid a heavy price. Linked by over 10 miles of tunnels was a heavily fortified system of cave and bunker complexes in which the Japanese hid 23 tanks, 430 artillery pieces, over 30 naval guns, 70 anti-tank guns, and 300 anti-aircraft guns. Initially they did not oppose the landing, but let US forces build up on the beach before opening up with everything they had and instigating a nightmarish bloodbath.

With air superiority and naval support the Marines stoically held their ground and slowly battled inland. Flamethrowers— whether the one-man M2 backpack or the Sherman M4A3R3 (known as Zippos or Ronsons after the cigarette lighters) proved vital to kill fanatical enemy soldiers who specialized in hiding then launching surprise attacks. The US Navy had an escort carrier sunk and two other ships badly damaged in a Kamikaze attack. On land US forces suffered 28,000 casualties and almost 7,000 killed. Of the approximately 21,000 Japanese only some 200 were taken prisoner. A third of the US troops committed to Iwo Jima (and again later at Okinawa) had been killed or wounded. These casualty statistics would be used to justify the later use of atomic weapons against the Japanese mainland, in order to save American lives.

Uparmored with concrete (note the white slab bottom right), this Sherman met its end during the battle of Iwo Jima. A 1945 report on the armored operations remarks, "There was much discussion as to whether or not certain area was tank terrain. The attitude of most of the tankers was that if they could get their tank in it and fire on the enemy, then it was tank terrain for them." Photo of sailors assigned to dock landing ship USS Harpers Ferry during the 62nd anniversary of the battle. US Navy photo by Mass Communication Specialist 3rd Class Mark R. Alvarez

Location: Ulsoor, India
Commemorating: Madras Engineering Group, whose sappers fought with the British Army in North Africa
Combatants: British Army; German Army
Date: 1941–1943

Below Right: *The Burma Star was awarded to Commonwealth personnel who fought in Burma.*

Far Right: *Maj Ezra Rhodes' M3 Grant of 2nd Infantry Division knocked out during the battle of Kohima.* Farhiz Karanjawala

Opposite: *The 225th anniversary of Madras Engineering Group saw this Stuart brought from North Africa to remember those who fought in the desert.* Mattlogelin

World War II Tanks in India

British Fourteenth Army is called the "Forgotten Army." Far away from the European Theater, fighting in the jungles of Burma, this was a huge army: nearly a million men, most from the Commonwealth, were fighting by the end of 1944. Eight Indian divisions, two West African, one East African and one British fought under Lt Gen Bill Slim, defending India from the Japanese before taking the offensive and retaking Burma. Many of the units went on to take part in the reoccupation of Malaya—unopposed, fortunately, after the Japanese surrender.

In the Arakan, at the battle of the Admin Box (February 5–23, 1944); around Kohima in Nagaland (April 4–June 22, 1944) and Imphal in Manipur (March 8–July 3, 1944), Fourteenth Army first held the Japanese and then, helped considerably by air support and air resupply, beat them. "When you go home, tell them of us and say, For your tomorrow, we gave our today" is carved into the memorial of the British 2nd Infantry Division in the CWGC cemetery at Kohima.

Armor played an important role in the campaign—particularly in the retaking of Burma and at the decisive battles of Meiktila and Mandalay (January–March 1945). Two Indian tank brigades (255th in Shermans and 254th in Grants and Stuarts) played an important role (as they would do in the Indo-Pakistan war of 1965 which saw many of WWII vehicles—Shermans, Grants, Stuarts, Chaffees—still on inventory).

Unsurprisingly, there are a number of preserved military vehicle collections and tank memorials around the subcontinent

STUART TANK-M5A1
BROUGHT BY MEG FROM NORTH
AFRICA WORLD WAR II, 1944.
PLACED HERE BY MEG ON
THEIR 225TH ANNIVERSARY.

271571

M4A1(76)W HVSS Sherman "Brownstown" Medium Tank

M4A1 (76)W HVSS SHERMAN "BROWNSTOWN"

Location: 101–199 Main St, Brownstown, Indiana, USA
Combatants: US Army
Commemorating: US Veterans of WWII
Date: 1939–1945

Unsurprisingly, as most of the Allied armor used in the war was built in America, there are many World War II-vintage armored vehicles visible in the United States, particularly around the many military installations and museums. This one is named after the small town in which it is placed, Brownstown in Jackson County on the courthouse lawn.

Its serial number identifies it as being built by the Pressed Steel Car Company sometime in July 1945. The exterior armored first aid box on the left hull side was introduced from April 1945 until the end of production. "Brownstown" is armed with a long-barrelled 76mm M1A2 main gun with a full muzzle brake, whose higher velocity gave a better performance for AP than the previous 75mm, although it did not perform as well with HE and this ultimately bred opposition in US military circles to its mass production.

"Brownstown" also has the HVSS with wider tracks to cope with the uparmoring increases in weight and allow a smoother ride. The Pressed Steel Car Company was the sole manufacturer of the M4A1(76)W HVSS, producing some 1,255 units from January until July 1945, so it is doubtful whether any saw combat in WWII. It also seems that any that were sent overseas returned: a 1948 US Army inventory lists the complete figure. The cast hull was in production longer than any other Sherman hull type with its improved large hatches and wet ammunition storage.

Post-WWII Israel bought almost 300 Shermans, including some M4A1(76)W HVSS, which formed the basis of the upgunned Israeli M50 and M51 Shermans.

Almost 50,000 Sherman tanks were built by ten US companies during WWII, making it the most-built Western tank of the war, behind only the Soviet T-34 (84,000).

Opposite: *"Brownstown" shows off its profile and HVSS.* Nyttend/WikiCommons

Left: *This Israeli M50 Super Sherman is on display at Beyt ha-Shiryon in Tel Aviv. It was originally built by Pressed Steel Car but upgunned using the French 75mm from the AMX-13. The M51 was the designation given to those Shermans upgunned with the French 105mm Modèle F1 gun. Because of the weight increases, HVSS Shermans were preferred, as were diesel engines.* Avi1111 dr. avishai teicher/WikiCommons (CC BY-SA 4)

M4A2 Sherman III "Bomb" Medium Tank

Right: *M4A2(76) HVSS "Boss" outside Beatty Street Drill Hall in Vancouver. A golden maple leaf on a green background indicates 4th Armoured Division; 53 indicates 28th Armoured Regiment—the British Columbia Regiment.* Sprinno/WikiCommons (CC0 1.0)

Far Right: *The war's over. It's June 8, 1945, and men of the Sherbrooke Fusiliers Regiment, are ready to go home. Their tank, "Boss," will travel home, too.* Department of National Defence. Library and Archives Canada, PA-188671

This M4A2 Sherman III, named "Bomb," was rescued from a Belgium junk heap and sent back to Canada, ending up at the town's Champs de Mars park. Following a decade long project to restore and relocate the tank it was then inagurated at the j99
on September 25, 2011. It has the distinction of being the last surviving Canadian fighting tank from the D-Day invasion, which fought from Normandy to Germany from June 1944 to May 1945 and survived two hits from enemy shells without being knocked out. It belonged to B Sqn of the 27th Armoured Regiment, also known as the Sherbooke Fusilier Regiment, and from its landing on Juno Beach on D-Day until VE-Day it covered 2,500 miles and fired 6,000 rounds.

The Sherman III designation indicates a Lend-Lease M4A2 Sherman, powered by a General Motors diesel 6046 engine and powertrain coming from the earlier M3A3/M3A5 Stuart tanks. The M4A2 was the first model manufactured with a welded hull and was used exclusively in Canadian armored regiments with the exception of a few Fireflies used to augment the anti-tank capabilities of the troops and squadrons. Both armored reconnaissance regiments of the 4th and 5th Armoured Divisions were also equipped with M4A2. In 1946, Canada purchased 300 M4A2(76)W HVSS vehicles and they were in use with the Canadian Army until replaced by the Centurion, and by reserve armored regiments in Canada as a training vehicle until the 1970s.

"Bomb" outside the William Street Armoury. HA/WikiCommons (CC BY-SA 4.0)

Bibliography

Chamberlain, Peter, and Ellis, Chris: *British and American Tanks of World War II*; Arms & Armour Press, 1977.

Ellis, John: *The World War II Databook*; BCA, 1993.

Forty, George: *Patton's Third Army at War*; Casemate Publishers, 2015.

Forty, George: *Tanks of World Wars I and II*; Southwater, 2006.

Forty, George: *World War Two Tanks*; Osprey, 1995.

Gaujac, Paul: *Dragoon The Other Invasion of France*; Histoire & Collections, 2004.

Jentz, Tom, Doyle, Hilary, and Sarson, Peter: *New Vanguard 5 Tiger I Heavy Tank 1942–1945*; Osprey, 1993.

MacDonald, Charles, B: *The Battle of the Bulge*; Weidenfeld, 1984.

Perrett, Brian, Smith, David E., and Chappell, Mike: *Vanguard 16 The PzKpfw III*; Osprey, 1980.

Perrett, Brian, and Smith, David E.: *Vanguard 21 The PzKpfw V Panther*; Osprey, 1981.

Senger und Etterlin, F.M. von: *German Tanks of World War II*; Arms & Armour Press, 1969.

Zaloga, Steve, and Sarson, Peter: *New Vanguard 3 Sherman Medium Tank 1942–1945*; Osprey, 1978.

Zaloga, Steve, and Sarson, Peter: *New Vanguard 9 T-34/76 Medium Tank 1941–1945*; Osprey, 1994.

Zaloga, Steve, and Sarson, Peter, and Badrocke, M.: *New Vanguard 57 M10 and M36 Tank Destroyers 1942–53*; Osprey, 2012.

Tank crew at Fort Knox, 1942. LoC

Index